Praise for
Sculpting the Business Body

"Through her interviews and observations, Karen has captured the true heart, soul, and actions required to be a successful entrepreneur."

Beverlee Rasmussen, Program Advisor, E-Myth Worldwide

"Relevant to anyone developing their business or aspiring to start one, *Sculpting the Business Body* is filled with practical, start-today strategies. Original and intelligent—a complete 'blueprint' for envisioning and creating a thriving business. Thanks to Karen's years of in-depth conversations with leading entrepreneurs, readers will come away with a deeper understanding of their entrepreneurial talents, skills and patterns of thinking."

Mary Ellen Sanajko, M.B.A., Executive Coach, Conduit Coaching; President, BNI Mountainside Chapter

"Karen McGregor's book is an entrepreneurial road map filled with insight, ideas and strategies. It captures the essence of the entrepreneur through interviews with those who have traveled the path to success."

Dayna Lalchun, M.B.A., Business Instructor

"*Sculpting the Business Body* is a brilliant celebration of entrepreneurial wisdom. Cleverly crafted, it's a light and easy read that is as entertaining as it is informative. Whether you're reading cover to cover or simply looking for a quick insightful tip, inspiration, or a call to action, this is a must-read for those on the entrepreneurial path."

Lynne Brisdon, Business Coach, Living in Vision Enterprises Inc.; Self-Employment Business Advisor, Toward Excellence Consulting Inc.

"It is great to see a fresh, honest approach. This book is an inspiration for new entrepreneurs, a guide for struggling entrepreneurs, and a friendly reminder for seasoned entrepreneurs."

Stan J. Tonoski, Executive Coach

Sculpting the
Business Body

Dai,
all the best
in business + life!

Sculpting the Business Body:

Strategies and Stories from Top Entrepreneurs

Karen McGregor

Behm Publishing
Langley, BC
Canada

Behm Publishing
4542-206A Street
Langley, B.C.
V3A 6L1
www.sculptingthebusinessbody.com

Library and Archives Canada Cataloguing in Publication
McGregor, Karen, 1968-
Sculpting the business body: strategies and stories from top entrepreneurs/Karen McGregor.
Includes bibliographical references.
ISBN 978-0-9781889-0-0
 1. Success in business—Canada. I. Title.
HF5386.M4746 2007   650.1   C2006-905712-5

Typesetting/publishing support: Kedre Murray, GF Murray Company
Cover design: Dotti Albertine, Albertine Graphic Design
Author photo: Victor Dezso, Victor Dezso Foto
Cover photo: Getty Images
Editing and proofreading: Sylvia Taylor, Taylor-Made Writing Services
Printed and bound in Canada by Friesens

To Dad,
the first entrepreneur in my life. I wish you were here.

Contents

x

Acknowledgments

I am blessed to have so many extraordinary people help me over the past two years in the writing of this book. Thank you so very much to the entrepreneurs who gave freely of their time and wisdom. Without you this book would not be possible. Thanks for the guidance, patience and professionalism of my graphic designer Kedre Murray and my editor and proofreader, Sylvia Taylor. You have made this book much better in so very many ways. Thank you, Dotti Albertine, for your creativity and resourcefulness in designing the cover.

It is important that I express my gratitude to the many women and men in my life who have enthusiastically given feedback at various stages of this book: Jodie Torhjelm, Kristy Cantin, Gay Brook, Stan Tonoski, David McLauren, Mary Ellen Sanajko, and John Oster. This book has evolved because of your guidance.

I would also like to acknowledge my dear friends who offered their support by taking care of my children while I worked to meet deadlines: Kristy Cantin, Sharon Delalla, Leanne Lim, Christine Bekar, and Trish Philpot. Mothers stick together and you've made the creation of this book possible.

To my husband Trevor and mother Marita, for your unconditional support, love and generosity during the writing of this book and always.

And lastly, thank you Matthew and Mitchell for your creative and energetic spirit. Mommy loves you up to the moon and back.

Introduction

Art enthusiasts come from every corner of our planet to see Michelangelo's *David*. Sculpted between 1501 and 1504, it is a formidable seventeen-foot image of Biblical David at the moment he decides to engage Goliath. What most people don't know is that Michelangelo's *David* differs from previous representations that depict the victorious David in the aftermath of the giant's defeat. Rather than celebrating, Michelangelo's *David* looks tense; his veins bulge from his lowered right hand and the twist of his body gives the impression that he is in motion. An apt metaphor for the budding entrepreneur—ready to act, sometimes merely in order to survive.

This book, however, is not just about survival or victory. Like Michelangelo and *The David*, it represents a journey of discovery and growth over time—a journey marked by challenges, defeats, celebrations, and epiphanies. Recreating King David must have been daunting for the twenty-six-year-old Michelangelo; two other sculptors had previously given up the task, despite being commissioned by the Operai, most of whom were members of the influential Wool Guild. The marble destined to be King David sat idle for two-and-a-half decades before Michelangelo was commissioned to complete the work.

In the early sixteenth century, prominent artists, including Leonardo Da Vinci, were consulted about what to do with the twenty-five-year-old slab of marble fondly called "The Giant". It was young Michelangelo, however, who was able to combine his communication and relationship skills with his talent, self-belief and conviction, to convince the Operai to employ him. Again and again, I heard similar stories of entrepreneurs who demonstrated these same skills—skills paramount to both daily successes and major turning points in their personal and professional lives. *The David* inside these entrepreneurs was revealed through years of diligence, as they continually defined and refined their work and themselves.

The image of sculpting was so clearly evident in my findings that it became the thread connecting the strategies and stories within this book. BC Forbes, founder of *Forbes* magazine, alludes to this image, echoing the perspectives of many entrepreneurs: "Think not of yourself as the architect of your career but as the sculptor. Expect to have to do a lot of hard hammering and chiseling and scraping and polishing." This action-oriented wisdom and the sculpting tools used to advance that action are the focus of this book.

While entrepreneurial sculpting tools come in different shapes and sizes, for the purposes of this book, they are grouped into three main parts. These parts are derived from two years of extensive interviews with 37 successful entrepreneurs from a variety of industries. Their conversations reveal four basic areas that are the foundation of business success, whether the entre-preneur *is* the business, or whether he or she employs hundreds of people. *Belief, awareness, relationships* and *systems*, were hailed as necessary in uncovering the Business Body—the person that, like *The David*, has always been there, and could use some sculp-ting tools to refine his or her business and entrepreneurial self.

In Part One, entrepreneurs discuss the form and shape of *belief*, and how they managed to strengthen belief over time.

Belief is the foundational rock the sculptor works with, and is integral to applying tools in the following part on *self and business awareness*. This part helps identify and clarify business direction, goals, strengths, values and attitudes. The questions and suggested activities up to this point are designed to be completed in the order presented; belief, state of mind and clarity about your future and what matters in your life, directly impact your communication skills and *relationships*, discussed in Part Three. The ability to relate well to others and form solid business relationships and connections is crucial to enduring business success. Chapter inclusions focusing on *systems* are placed strategically in various sections, helping you recognize different types of systems you can adopt or adapt in your pursuit of business excellence. To help you recall the entrepreneurs' businesses and accomplishments while reading these sections, biographies follow the conclusion.

Within the pages of this book, you will find much wisdom from people who have been through the roller-coaster-ride of becoming an entrepreneur. You will read the stories of people who overcame seemingly insurmountable obstacles and feel their moments of victory and joy. And perhaps, most important, you will come away with a course of action to grow or refine your own entrepreneurial skills. You might concentrate on relationship skills or refining systems of communication. You may focus on clarifying your vision and unique products and services. Or perhaps you want to develop psychological aspects of business, such as confidence, state of mind, and intuition. We are all different, and have different needs in our entrepreneurial journeys. It is my hope that you will use and re-use this book depending on your need at any given point in your journey.

Some stories and strategies will resonate with you, while others may be less impactful. This is natural, as you ultimately need to travel your own path after learning from others' experiences. Consequently, I have offered differing opinions and suggestions in order to help you create the plan of action best suited to your business and life. Also included, are my own personal stories that may resonate or provide possibilities for business action.

To encourage you to act on the wisdom within this book, there are thought-provoking questions, practical suggestions, and motivating quotes. Take time to reflect on your own learnings in each chapter, and create a plan of action. I have left space at the end of each chapter for this. To further your learning, a recommended reading list is provided in the bibliography.

One of Michelangelo's most famous discussions of his work involved visualizing *The David* within the marble. His belief was that the sculpture already existed inside the rock. All he had to do was reveal it to the world. In much the same way, this book is designed to reveal your entrepreneurial talents, skills, and patterns of thinking that will help you grow your business and move toward a rich, full life.

Take time to unveil *The David* within you.

Part One

Sculpting Belief

People become really quite remarkable when they start thinking that they can do things. When they believe in themselves they have the first secret to success.

Norman Vincent Peale

Chapter One

Belief to Action

Dozens of conversations with entrepreneurs revealed vivid images of the sculptor at work, chiseling, scraping and polishing creations with the help of specific tools. With no prodding on my part, most of the business owners talked about belief as *the* most essential tool when starting and growing a business. Without it, most said there would be no foundation upon which to succeed. But how does one acquire this belief? The answers varied, but many came back to six major themes:

▶ Belief of Others

▶ Common Threads of Passion and Skill

▶ Self-talk and Patterns of Thinking

▶ Victories Over Time

▶ The Cyclical Nature of Belief

▶ Purposeful Action

Belief of Others
Family

Many of the entrepreneurs talked about business-oriented family members being a significant force in their journey to self-belief. Little Caesars franchisee and real estate developer, Sandra Sereda, observed her parents' tremendous work ethic and entrepreneurial spirit in acquiring several farms. When they immigrated to Canada from Poland and Czechoslovakia, they had little, yet managed to carve their destiny through entrepreneurship. It was this fierce resolve and yearning for independence that Sandra, herself, developed at a young age. She recalls her unusual response to the "what do I want to do with my life?" section of her grade twelve graduation yearbook: "I want to be the president of my own company." Unusual because this response came in the early 70's, when many young women's aspirations were not geared to business, much less owning their own business. Yet Sandra's dream was to be independent and have total influence over her outcome. That she does, with 34 thriving restaurants, real estate developments and the launching of a healthy snack food, Tessa's Pita Chips.

Elana Rosenfeld, of Kicking Horse Coffee, says that she too attributes part of her self-belief to her parents. Because she watched her mother build a successful company of gourmet products from the ground up, the idea of owning a business wasn't foreign. In fact, Elana recalls being so entrepreneurial as a child that she would collect rocks off the street and try to sell them to neighbours! Later, when developing North America's first organic, gourmet coffee, Kicking Horse Coffee, she followed her mom's advice to keep her head up and chest out when going into sales meetings, and, if necessary, "fake it till you make it". This turned out to be wise advice for Elana, who learned that varying levels of self-confidence is part of the entrepreneurial journey.

Calling on family who really "get" what it means to be an entrepreneur also appears to ease the fears and doubts of business owners. For Darren McDowell of Just One Drop Water

Shops, being an entrepreneur can be lonely and frustrating. When Darren lacks belief in himself or has challenges to overcome, he calls his older brother, Walter, who understands the problems and opportunities involved in being an entrepreneur. Other entrepreneurs also connected with people whose attitudes and patterns of thinking encouraged self-belief. These supportive people gave helpful advice when asked, and recognized opportunity while understanding risk.

A few entrepreneurs who had entrepreneurial parents or family members, however, were reluctant about following in their footsteps. GO Get Organized owner, Tami Reilly, remembers being certain that she would never run her own business, due to watching her parents and grandfather run their various businesses, from one of Canada's first Dairy Queen and Kentucky Fried Chicken franchises, to a ski resort and hotel. She says she grew up lonesome because of the time they spent away from home, and came to believe entrepreneurship meant that work was all consuming, usually at the expense of family. However, when she married and had two children, she didn't want the life of a corporate executive either, so she made the decision to begin a home-based business, defining the parameters of her work to achieve a balance not witnessed as a child.

Real estate guru Ozzie Jurock credits his belief in himself to his mother, who told him he could do anything he wanted because he was an optimist. While he didn't realize the importance of her words as a child, he says, "I believed her. I believed her with a passion." This belief translated into Ozzie reaching and surpassing his goals on a yearly basis. In January of 2005, he and his partner set a goal to buy and sell 340 condos in twelve months. When I spoke to him in September of the same year, the goal had already been achieved.

Commercial real estate landlord and Brewmaster owner, Terry Smith, also spoke of family support as crucial to his belief and subsequent achievement of goals. When Terry graduated from high school in small-town Saskatchewan, he had few immediate goals and dreams to work toward. About to look for work on an oil rig, Terry was visited by his aunt, who sat him down, looked him square in the eye, and told him in no uncertain terms that he was going to university. She reminded him of his intelligence and potential, and the fact that he would be the first, and possibly only, member of their family to attend a post-secondary school. Relating this experience to me, Terry's eyes welled, thinking of the enormity of his aunt's talk—of the places it took him in life—from becoming a top sales executive with a large medical company to running his own businesses to becoming a city councilor and landlord.

We often hear that words have the power to change lives, but give little thought to how words shape and guide our personal lives. Don Miguel Ruiz, author of *The Four Agreements*, explains that as children, we believe everything adults say, and it controls our dream of life as we agree with the information passed on to us. Ruiz notes, "As soon as we agree, we believe it, and this is called faith. To have faith is to believe unconditionally." The majority of entrepreneurs interviewed were fortunate to have family that nurtured positive agreements, including: "You can do anything you want to," and, "You are unique and loved." While not all entrepreneurs shared this experience, those who did commented on its positive impact during their formative years and on into their first business ventures.

Third Circles and the Spark of Belief

It is amazing what other people believe you can do that you might otherwise limit yourself in.

Patti Fasan

For many entrepreneurs, acquaintances and even complete strangers changed their lives by strengthening their self-belief. Pizza franchisee, Sandra Sereda, says the most influential people in her development as a confident young business woman were two employers she had in her late teens and early twenties. She explains that their style of management, which encouraged creativity, responsibility and ownership, helped her self-belief blossom. In fact, when Sandra talks to her managers at Little

Caesars Pizza stores in Vancouver's Lower Mainland, she tells them of the influence managers can have in the lives of young employees:

> "If you, as the manager, are the controlling person, someone that puts others down and who doesn't give them the skills they need to become good, I think you're at a total disadvantage. Fortunately, I had two fabulous people I worked for who had total confidence in me and my abilities and gave me whatever I wanted to take on. They were instrumental in how I felt about myself and my self-confidence. They allowed me to say, 'Anything I want to do is accomplishable.' "

China King restaurant owner and venture capitalist, Eric Huang, had employers that gave him great opportunities to grow his managerial skills. In fact, they directly impacted his career direction, when, at age 22, he was promoted from an engineer to a manager of a large manufacturing company. Eric's employers saw his tremendous leadership abilities and allowed his strengths to blossom by giving the right person the right job. This promotion sparked confidence in Eric and he went on to work as a business consultant for the Chinese government.

In much the same way, Brenda Alberts, owner of Birthplace of B.C. Art Gallery, had someone recognize her strengths at a young age. She recalls being told by a high school councilor to reconsider her decision to become a teacher, like her sister, in favour of something that focused on her people-skills. This advice led Brenda through various secretarial jobs and retail experience, eventually culminating in ownership of an art gallery specializing in the original artwork of British Columbians. Her sales skills and long-term client development, combined with a genuine love of people, have helped Brenda survive in a business that most people said would never work.

A number of entrepreneurs met individuals who were in their lives for a brief time, yet were able to feed their self-belief. When freelance writer, Sylvia Taylor, first began planning her business, she took university writing courses to develop her skills and was seeking feedback about her submissions. Sylvia was called to speak with her instructor, a prominent writer and professor. What she said was etched in Sylvia's memory forever: "There are only three people I've told to become a writer. You're one of them." Sylvia wept with relief, recognizing that her friends and members of writing groups weren't just being "nice" in complementing her writing, but that she truly had the gifts and skills necessary to succeed. Sylvia has now developed her business to include, in her words, "all things writerly". Taylor-Made Writing Services, her company, edits manuscripts and magazines, produces articles and business writing, and offers writing courses.

Full-Circle Belief

This gift of belief comes full circle for many of the entrepreneurs, who take the time to say the words struggling, new entrepreneurs need to hear. Trent Dyrsmid, of Dyrand Systems, told of a time when he encouraged a young woman to become a realtor, and years later was told his words were a turning point in her life. She had become a highly successful realtor in Vancouver's Lower Mainland. When I asked Trent what his gift to the world is, I speculated that it might have something to do with his work, but his was a full-circle response: "To encourage and motivate entrepreneurs to begin working toward their dreams."

Ella Little, owner of a well-known boutique in Langley, British Columbia, is an encourager and motivator. When she speaks, people listen. No stranger to adversity, the newly-divorced mother of four moved from small-town Saskatchewan to Vancouver's Lower Mainland in 1976 with not much more than a 24-foot travel trailer to her name. Because of this financial and emotional hardship, Ella knows how much it means to others when they receive encouragement and advice. She never misses an opportunity to point out the talent in others, even when they don't yet believe in themselves. Up-and-coming designers like Karyn Chopik and Chloe Angus have been uplifted by Ella's belief and guided by her wisdom.

Leaders in self-development encourage people to use words that are positive and loving, first and foremost when talking and thinking about themselves. While I believe in this practice and challenge myself to embody this languaging, I am disheartened by adamant experts downplaying the influence others have in our self-confidence. In fact, these experts' proclamations differ from many of the entrepreneurs' perspectives. They did need someone else to believe in them in order to proceed with renewed hope.

A Note For Women

Because many of the women interviewed talked about their struggles to be seen as equal in the eyes of their male counterparts, they believed in being particularly supportive of women in business. Ceramic Tile Consultant Patti Fasan works almost exclusively with male executives and CEO's. Breaking into an "old boys' club" industry where women are not seen as experts was challenging. She explains that in the eyes of the Spanish and Italian aficionados of tile, "Men run ceramic tile companies, not women. Men know dirt and minerals and clay, not women. Not only do you have to be a man," she adds, "but you have to be in the industry for fifty years and your family has to have made ceramic tile since the thirteenth century." Patti's long journey to simply have her expertise validated has influenced her to believe that women often receive little support during difficult times, and could particularly use other women's support: "Women need more women to support and complement them. It helps build ourselves up. I look for excuses to complement women. It's not good enough just to think it."

Gail Evans expands on this philosophy in her book, *She Wins, You Win*. In this enlightening book, Evans says women are often viewed as a group, (unlike men, who are mostly seen as individuals in the workplace) and therefore the only way for women to succeed is to be supported by other women. She adds, "The only way to win is to take care of ourselves. And that means taking care of other women too, because that's how we will all succeed—when we take care of each other."

Common Threads of Passion and Skill

While most of the business owners were supported by family or acquaintances during their beginning years as entrepreneurs, a few had a difficult start to life, which did little to encourage entrepreneurial spirit. Maureen Wilson, owner of celebrity-acclaimed Sweat Co., had an absent, alcoholic father and unstable family life, moving many times over the course of her childhood. Maureen moved out on her own in her mid-teens, and was forced to learn survival skills. Because of this rude awakening to the world, it was a miracle she didn't travel the road of poverty, drug abuse or homelessness, like many other teenagers in similar situations. When I asked her what made the difference, her answer was simple and powerful: a clear vision of what she most needed to do in her life. Maureen knew deep down that she needed to do something physical, where she could use her energy in a meaningful way. By 19, she joined a fitness club and was so enthusiastic and committed to it, that after one month, she was asked to teach classes and take instructor training. A few years later, Maureen developed such confidence in her ability to train and connect with people on a personal level, she opened Sweat Co., an intimate, cozy workout studio that is a leader in hip alternatives to the Big Gym. She will soon celebrate her 25th anniversary there.

Unlike Maureen, Rob McGregor, co-owner of Spirit West, a change and perspectives consulting company, has had many careers in his life; from adult education, health care and home care, to being an administrator with social services and a budget officer for a government ministry. He is also qualified to be an Anglican minister. Many prospective entrepreneurs have similar experiences to Rob, in that they are well versed in a variety of skills, and particularly adept in dealing with diverse individuals and groups of people. Rob says, "There are a lot of things that make my heart sing. But the common thread across it all has been people. I love people." This love has made him a highly successful consultant, as his clients sense his caring and nonjudgmental nature. With this common thread weaving through his life, Rob has a strong belief in his abilities to connect on a deep level with individuals and companies.

Susan Rind, also in tune with what she most needs in life, was in her late teens when her mother asked her the big, "So what do you want to do with your life?" question. She immediately answered, "Something to do with my hands." This first took her to Switzerland, where she trained as an esthetician and landed a job in a world-renowned spa. As a young person in a foreign country, this could have been a particular trying time, but because of Susan's belief that she had a talent in using her hands, she flourished in the midst of a sophisticated and demanding clientele. Later, she became a hairstylist, a sales representative for hair products, and a painter of exclusive designs for women's wear, with the common thread of hand-work weaving through her life. Now as a jewelry designer, Susan is still happiest when she is creating—using her hands to fulfill a primary need.

Consider This

▶ If you are a prospective entrepreneur who isn't sure what type of business to develop, examine the common thread amongst jobs, hobbies or special moments that bring you joy. This may guide you to the type of business you want to dedicate your time and energy to. Marketing expert, Wendy McClelland, suggests women seeking career or business direction recall what they loved to do at the age of eight or nine. Such an exercise excavates our innate gifts and passions, and strengthens self-belief, as we are reminded of our talents and great joys in life.

▶ What do you NEED, mentally, emotionally, physically or spiritually when working? Need, as opposed to want—something integral to your nature, to the part of you that makes you unique,

the part that makes your heart sing. List what you
need to be fulfilled. How can you incorporate this
need into your business, turning it into a primary
strength?

Self-Talk and Patterns of Thinking

Although some of the people interviewed didn't have significant
others or family to boost their self-confidence, they all used
positive self-talk. While this may be one of the most difficult
ways of sustaining belief, magazine publisher and renowned
speaker, Peter Legge, suggests that people pay close attention
to what they say about themselves and to what thoughts
repeatedly enter their minds—thoughts that, over time, can build
or erode self-belief. Once aware of these thoughts, the process
of change can begin.

Financial consultant, Alphonse Seward, works on his mental
state by being aware of the times he is going down the well-
traveled path of negativity. By doing so, he is able to stop himself
and redirect thoughts. This monitoring of internal dialogue is
helpful in that it is the first step in regaining optimism. Jacqueline
Jongkind, a top executive of a direct-sales company, uses the
image of a light switch to immediately replace destructive
thoughts. "Flip your switch," she advises other entrepreneurs.
Her metaphor has worked for me as well, making me realize
that I have the power to turn the light on or remain in the
darkness, paralyzed with self-induced negativity.

Omitting certain words entirely from thoughts and the
spoken word is also part of the awareness of how we talk to
ourselves. Tami Reilly says, she avoids "what if's" altogether, not
allowing herself to become focused on the idea of failure. In
What to Say When You Talk to Your Self, Shad Helmstetter says
we need to take this awareness of thought patterns one step
further, creating new words and sentences at the exact moment
that we catch ourselves in negativity. Helmstetter explains that
it is as if the human brain is saying: "Give me more. Give the

words. Give me the directions, the commands, the picture, the schedule, and the results you want. Then I will do it for you. Give me the words."

Helmstetter reassures his readers that the positive way we talk to ourselves is no longer considered a success theory, but is fact: "Neither luck nor desire has the slightest thing to do with it. It makes no difference whether we believe it or not. The brain simply believes what you tell it most. And what you tell it about you, it will create. It has no choice." This idea of saying the very thing we don't yet believe may seem strange at first, yet with enough repetition and small daily actions toward our goals, belief strengthens. Most people wait until they believe they can do something before they attempt doing it, yet research shows merely thinking about and announcing our intentions goes a long way towards the realization of dreams.

International speaker Azim Jamal not only sees the results of this in his self-belief, but also in his family's belief in him. For several years, he has been saying out loud, "I am one of the top ten speakers in the world. I've sold at least 5.7 million copies of my books." Because he says this daily as though it has already come to fruition, his eleven-year-old son, Tawfiq, believes that this is reality. During career day at school, Tawfiq reported that his dad was one of the top ten speakers in the world. Azim explains that, "He thinks it's true because that's how he sees me walk, talk, breathe, act, speak. And so it becomes a self-fulfilling prophecy. And he hears me every morning and every night, loudly in my prayers, that Azim is this, this and this. So he believes it."

For Azim, there is a firm belief that "talking and acting as if the goal has already been achieved sets the intention clearly out to the Universe, which attracts the right people and circumstances" in his life. Not surprisingly, Azim is well on his way to fulfilling his vision, having co-authored the international bestselling book, *The Power of Giving*, and having addressed over a million people while sharing the stage with some of the world's most influential thinkers, including Dr. Deepak Chopra and Dr. Wayne Dyer.

Consider This

▶ Find some solitary time (try starting with fifteen minutes) to simply become fully aware of your thoughts; thoughts that help or hinder the achievement of vision and goals. Try recording your negative thoughts and replacing them with specific, supportive ones. For instance, if you think, "I'll only ever get customers in the small area I live in," flip your switch with "I attract customers from across the province or state, and in five years, I will have retail stores in three other provinces or states."

▶ When you do encounter thoughts that hinder, acknowledge the person that you once were, rather than berating yourself for not changing in an instant. Executive Coach, Mary Ellen Sanajko, also suggests treating yourself gently and starting slowly—otherwise, it's like learning to ride a bike on a mountain.

Victories Over Time

Several entrepreneurs drew from past experiences, business-related or otherwise, to feed their entrepreneurial spirit with belief. When marketing expert, Wendy McClelland, talks about the origins of her belief, she dates it back to the year her mother passed away. Eight-year-old Wendy took on the role of raising her three younger siblings while her father worked. She did most of the family planning and took her brother and sisters to appointments and lessons. While today this would seem like a tremendous burden for such a young girl, Wendy says, "It showed me that I could do things that other people wouldn't expect an eight-year-old to do." This confidence led her to aspire to be the first woman prime minister, but when she began her university training in law, she became bored (a common remark by many of the entrepreneurs when discussing schooling and post-secondary education) and quickly recognized her need for a different challenge. At nineteen, Wendy incorporated her first business and immediately felt at home as an entrepreneur. She has owned and operated several more successful businesses since then, including a parenting magazine, an on-line business resource centre, and her current on-line marketing business, Think Without Boundaries.

Trent Dyrsmid, owner of Dyrand Systems, a virtual IT company, says he developed self-confidence mainly by recognizing his strengths when he began working as a stockbroker. He excelled in sales, and thought if he was great at sales maybe he could start his own business selling something. After incorporating Dyrand Systems and partnering with its current president, Ed Anderson, Trent began making cold calls every day for two years. Trent's results led him to say to himself, "If I can create my own business with strong sales, I can create a different type of business and sell different products." This is precisely what he did with his Internet-based jewelry company, quickly producing lucrative passive income.

Eric Huang, venture capitalist and owner of China King restaurant, had a similar experience to Trent's in that he gained confidence early in his career by working for a large American grocery chain, expanding their in-store Chinese restaurants from one to twenty-three in three years. This success, coupled with his increasing command of the English language and adoption of a more aggressive American culture, led him to invest $200,000 (his life's savings) to develop his own Chinese restaurant in Canada. The success of China King then led him to create a Chinese newspaper, and most recently, a business financing and consulting firm.

The awareness of talents and skills through life and work experiences provides the foundation of belief for many other entrepreneurs I spoke with. Laura Prosko, owner of an event-planning and public relations company, says her confidence skyrocketed after raising over $72,000 for a band to tour across Canada and the eastern US. She arranged for press and publicity, and said to herself, "I'm entrepreneurial. If I can do this, I can start a business." A couple of years later, she opened Prosko Group Productions Inc., and has put on many newsworthy events, including a rock n' roll gala for the AIDS Foundation and numerous events for politicians.

Similarly, Brian Takeda, at the age of 24, started up *muzi tea bar* with a solid belief in himself that had little to do with his Queens University business education. At the age of six, Brian was performing piano concerts and was later considered semi-professional. These performances gave him a level of confidence in front of groups that would never leave him. (This echoes the experience of many other entrepreneurs, who felt their public leadership, music, or athletic abilities and competitions, significantly impacted their confidence levels.)

In his youth, however, Brian had his fair share of challenges. For several years after emigrating from Japan, he struggled in school, often not understanding what teachers were saying. At age thirteen, he got help from an English teacher who reconstructed his language skills, and he went on to win a debating competition at Harvard. As a teenager, Brian also struggled with obesity, and remembers deciding that if he was going to have a chance with the girls, he better do something about it. After losing over 30 pounds, Brian knew that if he could do that, he could do anything.

Although belief is noted as a choice and an attitude in many self-development books, my findings showed that it stemmed more from victories, small and large; from the actions entrepreneurs took to prove to themselves they were capable of doing what it takes to succeed. While they remembered past victories as a way to feed belief, they simultaneously proceeded with action.

Consider This

▶ Belief, in some shape and form, begins long before you become an entrepreneur. What successes have you had in different areas of your life?

▶ Record successes on a time line, whether they seem significant or not. Look at how they play a role in your life today. Our successes reveal our talents, skills, passions, and strength of will, and help build the foundation of belief necessary to take risks in starting and growing a business.

The Cyclical Nature Of Belief

What self-development experts often downplay is that self-belief, even in the most successful, balanced, joyful people, can fluctuate given certain triggers, circumstances, and situations. Executive Performance Coach, Peri Shawn, helps clients move their business forward, and knows that for many people, belief is not a constant:

"We have ups and downs, and need to recognize and expect that. To think that we will always feel good about ourselves is unrealistic, because we face challenges every day and a normal part of life is to doubt. If you don't doubt, then you're probably not living. So acknowledge its existence and then don't let it stop you."

One of the first challenges to a new entrepreneur's belief is the emotional attachment to their old job and old self. "Being an entrepreneur is not a job or career, it's a way of life," says Speakers' Spotlight CEO, Farah Perelmuter. When you join the world of entrepreneurship, you are not only leaving your job, but you are beginning a new journey, where you are completely responsible for your professional and personal welfare.

This transition from employee to entrepreneur, Maureen Fitzgerald notes, is a difficult one, "because you do make a decision at some point whether or not you really believe you can make it." Maureen, president of CenterPoint Inc., tore up her certificate to practice law, saying that she needed to do it in order to make the commitment to her entrepreneurial consulting business clear and tangible. (For future contract work as a consultant, however, Maureen taped it back together!)

There is often a moment in this process when entrepreneurs recognize their self-growth and that of their business, but are tempted to revert back to the safety of old ways of being. This might include sabotaging themselves with destructive thoughts or actions, such as procrastination, showing up late for meetings, and not doing what they said they would do. Sound familiar? This is, in fact, a common experience amongst entrepreneurs. Author and motivational speaker Og Mandino expresses it poetically in *The Greatest Miracle in the World*: "Even those few who risked their future in order to advance still found it necessary to constantly fight that compelling urge to flee back to their previous womb of security no matter how bleak their old existence had been."

Part of the budding entrepreneur may feel resistance from those closest to them. Alphonse Seward remembers feeling a tug to go back to his family-owned renovation company because that's where friends and family were familiar with his old ways of being. Like other interviewees, Alphonse notes that most people accepted his new way of life after a period of time. Unfortunately, some of those interviewed were disappointed in colleagues, friends or spouse who were unable to graciously move on and embrace the changes.

Consider This

▶ I often hear beginning entrepreneurs voice concerns over a lack of family or peer support, dreading the, "I told you so," from 'experts' at work or at home. In saying "no" to the naysayers, ask yourself, "What am I saying 'yes' to?" What does that make possible?

Purposeful Action

Trent Dyrsmid of Dyrand Systems says, that at some point, belief and the transition to entrepreneur must translate into action, and it is in the small, daily actions that our belief takes shape.

Physically, mentally and emotionally, we feel better when we move. Momentum creates confidence. Trent races cars as a hobby. No doubt even this "play" part of his life influences and satisfies a need for momentum, for challenge, furthering his confidence in all areas of life.

Brian Scudamore's entire business embraces this philosophy, not just for employees and franchisees, but also for customers. The founder and CEO of 1-800-GOT-JUNK?, Brian's motto is "Just Get It Done", encouraging customers to simply act to rid themselves of the junk impeding their lives.

▶ My Story: Why It's Necessary to Make the Transition

I had a vivid dream once in which I stood, paralyzed, in a dimly lit hallway. I could see a room in front of me and a room behind me, and was fearful to enter either one, preferring the safety of the corridor. A shadowy figure suddenly appeared, attempting to wrestle me to the ground, but each time it tried, I pinned it to the floor. Once I finally managed to do away with it, it would spring back up and attack me again. I woke up in the middle of one of these battles, sweating, and realized I had met the monster of transition—I didn't move forward to the room ahead of me yet couldn't bear to look at the room behind me—my past. I realized at that moment two things: one, the shadowy figure would continue to get up if I remained in the hallway, and two, I had to move into the unknown to deal with the fear and live a full life. I remember listening to Tony Robbins say no relationship is static, which is why you have to work on it. If you do nothing to make your marriage better, it gets worse. If you do nothing to improve your confidence, your sense of self, it too deteriorates. Living in the hallway is living a life of deterioration.

The Inexplicable
Advantages of Action

In many studies and in my discussions with successful entrepreneurs, there is much evidence that action is correlated with synchronicity and creativity. Some people believe that creativity comes only to the fortunate or gifted, and that synchronicity is just a fantasy that exists in the minds of New Age business people. Studies show that moving out of our heads and into our bodies and the world generates more ideas and more favorable coincidences. So while our mental activities, like reading, research and journaling are beneficial, the inexplicable happenings that move our business along often occur when we initiate action.

Trent Dyrsmid illustrates this, when he had been thinking of starting a second business selling women's products, and began calling individuals who had lucrative Internet businesses. One entrepreneur, after guiding Trent through the ins-and-outs of setting his business up to be successful, casually recommended that Trent consider selling women's jewelry on-line. A few minutes later, Trent walked out of his office and down the hall to a supplier of handbags, where he requested product information that might help him plan his new business. He was given a supplier's catalogue that happened to include a feature article on fashion jewelry. Trent says, "It was like the bolt of confirmation that I was heading down the right path. What are the odds that I'm going to get off the phone, and twenty minutes later, not one hundred feet in front of me, I'm given a magazine with the feature article on exactly what the guy had suggested to me, which fit everything I'd been thinking about for the past twelve months?" Yet, Trent's action was necessary to set the synchronistic event in motion.

Too many people sit on their thoughts and ideas, waiting for "the right time", when all the coordinates of the universe are aligned to guarantee success. It is our action that sets in motion the inexplicable happenings that propel our business forward. Spiritually speaking, our action is rewarded on a higher plane. You've likely heard the now commonplace mantra, "the

Universe rewards action." The people who really believe it are the people that take action; they have been witness to the frequent coincidence, the lovely message that they are not alone.

Those whose work involves artistic creativity also experience the principle of action being rewarded by our Universe. For freelance writer Sylvia Taylor and jewelry designer Susan Rind, the creative juices only flow when there has been a great deal of "doing". Perspiration before inspiration. For those who accept and act on this reality, creativity is an example of the Principle of Abundance. Award-winning writer and activist, Maya Angelou, explains, "You can't use up creativity. The more you use, the more you have."

Wisdom in Action

Do not let what you cannot do interfere with what you can do.

John Wooden

Something in human nature causes us to start slacking off at our moment of greatest accomplishment. As you become successful, you will need a great deal of self-discipline not to lose your sense of balance, humility and commitment.

H. Ross Perot

Sometimes our light goes out, but is blown into flame by another human being. Each of us owes deepest thanks to those who have rekindled this light.

Albert Schweitzer

Write down three points of action you will take after reviewing this chapter. Then reflect on the quotes above and how these words translate to action in your life.

Chapter Two

What Drives You? Passion, Purpose and Protest

While entrepreneurs talked about the basic importance of action, the inevitable questions of motivation came to mind. What motivates entrepreneurs to act? What keeps them going over the long haul? While I knew that motivation moves people to act, often resulting in greater self-belief, I was surprised that motivations were so diverse. From righting social injustices to following life-long passions, motivations were as individual as the entrepreneurs themselves.

Different motivations were equally successful in helping entrepreneurs commit and follow through on their vision and goals. Some motivations, however, changed as entrepreneurs made transitions from their first years to their first decade in business. Many of the entrepreneurs, for example, viewed money as a primary motivator early on in their businesses, but not after the first few years. Their motivators through the peaks and valleys of entrepreneurism include:

▶ Creation

▶ Impact on Others

▶ A Passion for People

▶ Purpose

▶ Fun

▶ Naysayers

▶ Financial Challenges

Creation

This is the motivator of the 'Donald Trumps' of the world: to put something into existence that wasn't there before, and turn it into a world-class company. When I asked entrepreneurs whether they would consider developing new businesses, many of them said yes, primarily due to this natural desire to create. Trent Dyrsmid says he's learned in the past four years that his passion is in the creation of companies, rather than in the running of them. He explains that, "If it requires me to run it, it's a job. If it runs without me, it's a business." His passion is coming up with an idea, doing the initial research on it, and turning it into a system that uses profit sharing to reward the people running it.

Sandra Sereda can relate to this desire for creation. A co-owner of 34 Little Caesars Pizza franchises, Sandra's recent milestone birthday saw her reflect on her life and begin visualizing her deepest entrepreneurial wish—to take a concept from inception to finished product. While she still helps operate the pizza stores, her need for creation urged her to develop a product called Tessa's Pita Chips, scheduled to hit Western Canadian retail stores by the Fall of 2006. She also began looking at real estate opportunities in Western Canada, partnering in a large parcel of land for future subdivision and purchasing recreational properties on speculation. Some of the properties were sold for double the purchase price less than two years later. Her friends believe she's a money-magnet, with everything she touches turning to gold. But for Sandra, the real motivation is using her gifts and skills to work through the challenges and see the creation unfold.

Other entrepreneurs took great pleasure in helping their companies grow, and had great passion for working through challenges. While I interviewed George Preston, an architect who built Preston Chevrolet asked, "Retiring anytime soon?" George smiled and said, "Retire? I love it too much to retire." At 74, George simply enjoyed doing things well. He added, "I like to have things grow properly, just like a garden." When I heard of George's passing in January of 2006, I thought he would be pleased with the magnificent garden he left behind.

One surprise in my findings was that creation often became a much greater motivator than passion for a particular product or service. Colin Bosa, president of Bosa Properties, says he has always been interested in building homes and high rises, but his real passion is in building a world-class company. Colin compares this passion to an executive with 1-800-GOT-JUNK?, who said, "I don't love junk. I love 1-800-GOT-JUNK?"

When Rick and Jacqueline Jongkind became partners in a direct-selling business, they had two very different reasons for doing so. Rick saw the enormous potential to create the lifestyle of his dreams, while Jacqueline saw the high-quality products as incentive to grow the business. Similarly, when Wally Garrick co-founded All Weather Shelters ten years after his fish and tackle store failed, fishing remained his first love. He did, nevertheless, see the demand for outdoor mobile shelters, and it was only then that he discovered his enthusiasm for using problem-solving skills to create custom shelters for a growing clientele in the oil and gas industry. In today's marketplace, where passion is preached as a must, prospective entrepreneurs often consider only those products or services they have an avid interest in. This seems to make natural sense, yet many of the entrepreneurs I spoke with say that their radar is out for other business opportunities because they love the challenge of growing a business.

Impact on Others

Several entrepreneurs were clearly motivated by the impact their business would have on others, from charitable causes to creating employment to motivating and mentoring. I was amazed by the host of inspiring stories entrepreneurs shared—stories which illustrated causes much bigger than any one individual. One such story comes from Azim Jamal, who visited Karachi and was witness to abject poverty and tales of violence: fathers unable to provide food and clothing for their children, children who watched their fathers being killed. Such dire conditions spurred his commitment to those in desperate circumstances. Through his philanthropic giving and promotion of his book, *The Power of Giving*, Azim creates the ripple-effect of purpose.

Rick Jongkind, a top executive for a direct-sales company, says his motivation first came from wanting to create a lifestyle for his family where money would no longer be a primary concern. What he and his wife Jacqueline most wanted was more family time and enough money to create wonderful memories with their children and in their marriage. Similarly, GO Get Organized president, Tami Reilly, decided to begin her own business rather than work her way up the corporate ranks—she knew her children needed to come first in her life. Like many entrepreneurial women, Tami decided to run her own business because she wanted the flexibility of choosing her work hours. Yet Tami's perception of entrepreneurs came from her father and grandfather, who worked day and night with no time for family. Tami struggled with vivid memories of being a child alone at home while her family worked. Not wanting this life for her own children, she arrived at a viable solution: "I decided that if I was going to work for myself, I would have to decide the parameters of how it would all come together ... How would I do this differently? How would I make it work for me? So I made a list of criteria I needed it to be and then I made a list of things I didn't want it to be. And I just started looking for that first list of things."

Tami's story speaks to many parents who want to spend more time with their children and aren't looking for the get-rich-quick schemes. She says, "I'm sacrificing the big money-rush right at the beginning. I'm going for the slow burn because I'm fitting this into my life; it's not the other way around." She uses an elevator to describe the different paths people take, and that hers was not the elevator she had expected to take. I asked her if her elevator was one that meandered and took frequent stops (thinking of my own children and the writing of this book) and she replied, "No, it's still straight up. It's just a different elevator." I loved this perspective and began looking at my life in a different light; appreciating my relationships and work rather than what I'm not getting done on any particular day. The elevator is indeed different, but it is an elevator, and it's still going in the right direction.

A Passion for People

Passion for work was a common theme during the interviews, and many of the entrepreneurs urged others to be passionate about their work. But it was the passion for people that was highlighted even more. Owner of an exclusive women's boutique, Ella Little had always had a love of high fashion and good quality clothing. Later as an entrepreneur, she discovered an equally motivating passion: her customers. She notes that these women all have a story to tell, and that it has been her greatest source of joy to work with and serve women.

Patti Fasan took a leap of faith, leaving her job as Director of a large ceramic tile company to become an independent consultant and speaker, specializing in the history, architecture, and installation of ceramic tile. Patti says the reason she left her high-paying job was because she spent so little time with clientele and more and more time doing solitary office work. With the help of her husband, who noticed her growing unhappiness, she recognized her primary need to work with people wasn't being met. Patti now travels extensively across Europe and North America, earning far more than she did as an executive, and, more importantly, reclaiming her passion of helping people learn and grow.

George Preston was the perfect model of the businessman with a passion and purpose for the people in his life. At the time that I interviewed him, he had over 100 employees working at his car dealership. He proudly introduced me to most of them and told me not only what they contributed to the company, but also a little bit about their personal lives. It was obvious that every employee loved George as they laughed with him and beamed when he praised their abilities. The feeling was mutual.

After witnessing many entrepreneurs admire and praise the employees they work with, I have come to believe the people we surround ourselves with directly impact our passion, or lack thereof, for work.

Purpose

In Jack Canfield's *The Success Principles*, he notes, "Everything you do should be an expression of your purpose ... Without purpose as the compass to guide you, your goals and action plans may not ultimately fulfill you." Marketing expert, Wendy McClelland, among other entrepreneurs, believes that her life's purpose is motivating and inspiring others to follow their dreams. Whether giving keynote speeches, seminars, coaching, or leading through the example of her own entrepreneurial ventures, Wendy has inspired many business owners to reach their goals. She has even given hope to kids, sharing the story of an eighteen-year-old boy, who, inspired by her message of no-limit thinking and acting, said that no one had told him before that he could accomplish what he most wanted in life. And what Wendy provides is not empty motivational talk—she knows what it's like to face insurmountable odds. Having had several severe health complications, including a near-death experience with *E. coli*, she has rebounded to create a lucrative business and life for herself and her three children. A sense of purpose helped her get there.

Because I experienced the power of purpose in my own life and read motivational books that insisted everyone have a significant reason for investing their time, energy and talents, I assumed that the people I interviewed would speak of the importance of purpose. Yet over half of the entrepreneurs I spoke with did not see purpose as their primary motivator. Boutique owner, Ella Little, says, "I don't feel like I have any huge purpose in my life, but I've been a part of a lot of people's very important times in life. I haven't been there, but I've been able to make them ready to go. That's been fun." Ella responded the way most of the entrepreneurs did when asked about their purpose—with a humble acknowledgement that they have positively influenced the lives of others.

It's worth noting that purpose can only be a motivator if you are supplying a service or product that people want and are willing to pay for. Unfortunately, many entrepreneurs are motivated to make a difference, but eventually discover that their business is not financially viable. Frederick Buechner defines purpose wisely by saying that it is "the place where your deep gladness meets the world's needs." Prospective entrepreneurs would do well to continually keep this at the forefront while researching and planning their businesses.

Consider This

▶ Some people believe their business must have an existential reason behind its creation, a lofty purpose to support its existence. I have found there are several valid motivators that would not be considered noble by most, but nonetheless provide entrepreneurs with sufficient drive. Fun, the words of naysayers, and financial challenges all gave entrepreneurs the motivation they needed at different points in their business ventures.

Fun

Yes, pure and simple. Business success from a financial standpoint allows people to have fun when they're not working. This fun, for some, is a primary motivator in life. Trent Dyrsmid loves racing cars. In order to do that, he needs money... and lots of it. Money that comes from creating and building successful businesses. Because of his focus on fun, Trent is relaxed and one of the most balanced businessmen I know. He never works more than a forty-hour workweek, even when his business was struggling in the first year-and-a-half. So much for the theory that the entrepreneur must sacrifice everything in life for the business.

While Trent works to play, some of the entrepreneurs talked about play at work. John Stanton of the Running Room is playing when he runs with customers, gives motivational and informational talks, and promotes new books and products. He says that when people ask him how many hours per week he works, it's difficult to answer, because for him, work is play and play is work. It is this perspective that is a frequent motivator in building businesses over the long haul.

Like John, Brian Scudamore has been in business for almost two decades and looks forward to going to work daily. As the Founder and CEO of one of Canada's biggest franchises, Brian has stamped fun into the very essence of 1-800-GOT-JUNK? Because he believes in the value of fun at work, he has gone to great lengths to create a culture of fun. One example comes from his marketing department, which created the now famous Blue Wig Campaign. Combining energy and passion with laughter and light-heartedness, Brian has his drivers wearing blue wigs at promotional events and marketing activities. When thousands of blue wigs were handed out to Vancouver Canuck fans during a playoff game, the stadium went wild, with the wigs in hot demand for the remainder of the season.

Consider This

▶ Fun can be a source of motivation for employer and employee. Too often the new entrepreneur becomes burned out, out of balance, and misses raising their children and being with friends and family because they think fun is not necessary and even unprofessional. Some of the happiest, most peaceful entrepreneurs are those who consistently engage in activities other than their

businesses. And yes, they are also making the Big
Bucks.

▶ What is the role of fun in your life? What would
be available to you if you had more fun? What
would that make possible?

▶ In what ways does fun impact your employees?
How can you work at the fun quotient in your
business so that it promotes healthy relationships,
creativity, and balance?

Naysayers

A few months ago, I had the privilege of hearing cancer-survivor
and champion cyclist Lance Armstrong talk about a turning point
in his life when he was told he had cancer and would not likely
survive it. As the doctor gave him the prognosis and he watched
his mother cry for the first time in his life, Lance made a decision
to prove the medical experts and cyclist enthusiasts wrong by
making a comeback—a comeback that would see him not only
beat cancer, but go on to win the pinnacle of every cyclist's dream:
the Tour de France. Stunned, naysayers watched as year after
year he dominated the competition, winning it seven times before
retiring. In a keynote speech, Lance attributed much of this
drive to proving these naysayers wrong.

The motivation to prove others wrong is also alive and well
in the world of business. Several men and women admitted that
naysayers were a primary source of motivation, particularly, early
on in their business. Wendee Lynn Cristante, founder of
Canadian Clyde Ride, was told she wasn't knowledgeable
enough, smart enough, or "male" enough to pull off her dream.
The more the naysayers talked, however, the more Wendy was
determined to make the Clyde Ride a reality. When she was
invited to perform with her team at the 2005 Rose Bowl, Wendee
Lynn knew she had finally proved everyone wrong. Her new
motivation took its seeds from the Rose Bowl, where she and
her Canadian team were treated by the mainly American

audience with great respect and fanfare. Overwhelmed with the lavish response, she saw the opportunity to instill more national pride in Canadians through the Clyde Ride. Today, this is her primary mission. As she and each member of her team carry the Canadian flag with their Clydesdales decked out in red and white, it is easy to see how her mission will become a reality as the Clyde Ride develops legendary status.

Other entrepreneurs discussed the necessary and taxing difficulty involved in acting despite naysayers. Patti Fasan advises entrepreneurs to hold fast to goals, saying that "Because they (naysayers) can't imagine it, doesn't mean you can't make it successful." Ken Funk, former owner and president of Golden Valley Foods, tells a story of a naysayer who presented him with dismal data in an effort to protect him from the reality that he could never sell jam in Edmonton. Ken said, "I had just one problem. I didn't believe him." Golden Valley Foods was sold during the writing of this book, and one of its most prized possessions was jam products, sold across Canada, even in Edmonton.

Pizza franchisee Sandra Sereda brought up an interesting perspective that sometimes it's not others, but the doubting voice inside us, that becomes our personal naysayer. This can be defeating for many people, but for Sandra, it was sufficient motivation to prove to herself that she could move into unfamiliar territory and still build a successful business: "I hate to think that I can't do something. So if there's an obstacle, I say, 'I know someone that can help me with that. There's got to be some-thing I can do.'" Sandra's great desire to prove the doubting-self wrong has led her to become the business woman she is today.

Financial Challenges

For Eric Huang, fear of indefinite financial struggle drove him to entrepreneurship. The venture capitalist, business consultant, and owner of China King, says that just months after immigrating to Canada, he realized the way to wealth was to become an entrepreneur. With an MBA under his belt and years of managerial expertise, Eric felt disgruntled with his position as a manager of a fast-food chain. The pay was dismally low and advancement opportunities did not promise financial freedom— part of his definition of success. He decided to invest his life-savings in a restaurant similar to many he had opened for a company in the U.S. China King has provided quality food to patrons for over eight years, and has afforded Eric his goal of financial freedom, enabling him to provide financial assistance to other businesses.

For many of the entrepreneurs interviewed, the fear of succumbing to debt in the early stages of their business was a key motivator in taking action. Darren McDowell, owner of Just One Drop Water Shops, says, "When you are in a stressful situation, where you're forced into a corner, the human spirit, all your gifts and strengths, will click." Similarly, Trent Dyrsmid notes, "It is amazing the motivation that comes from being deeply in debt. And the focus, and the perseverance."

Former schoolteacher, Ken Funk, took the jam-side of his father's Golden Valley Foods business from the confines of his mother's kitchen to a multi-million dollar success. Knowing nothing about business, Ken had one thing going for him: fear of failure. He says, "The fear of failure got me up in the morning, got me to work. I had a real desire to make it. Whatever it took, I would do it."

Consider This

▶ While conventional wisdom says negative sources of motivation rarely work, many individuals who have lucrative businesses relied on these sources in their first years. In time, most of the negative motivation was replaced by a clear purpose and vision. If you are a beginning entrepreneur, know that different motivations work at different times in your business' development.

Wisdom in Action

The greatest use of life is to spend it for something that will outlast it.

William James

Do just once what others say you can't do, and you will never pay attention to their limitations again.

Edmund Brown, Jr.

Keep away from people who try to belittle your ambitions. Small people always do that, but the really great make you feel that you, too, can become great.

Mark Twain

Write down three points of action you will take after reviewing this chapter. Then reflect on the quotes above and how these words translate to action in your life.

Chapter Three

Dealing with Risk, Dealing with Failure

Because some conversations I had with entrepreneurs focused on the necessity of belief and the motivations that strengthen belief and commitment, I assumed that fear would be a non-issue in their lives, particularly for those with decades of business experience. What I discovered was not a superhuman quality, but authentic voices admitting that fear of failure never goes away. Sandra Sereda voices a common theme amongst many entrepreneurs, saying that although she may be confident, "Don't for a minute think that there aren't days when I wake up and think, 'I can't do this.' Because there are those days. Everyone has those days." Sandra's honesty in voicing her insecurities was a stark contrast to many self-development gurus whose advice of the day suggests that entrepreneurs (and anyone else who dares to dream) must develop an unwavering belief in themselves in order to reach their goals and vision. The problem with such advice is that it discourages people from working through problems; the moment fear creeps in, they tell themselves they don't have what it takes to be in business. Suggestions I gleaned from entrepreneurs centred on five practical and motivating points:

▶ Refining Perspectives on Failure

▶ Recognizing Gifts

▶ Tapping into Spiritual Beliefs

▶ Stretching Comfort Zones

▶ Studying the Numbers

Refining Perspectives on Failure

Acceptance of fear works well for many entrepreneurs. Along with this acceptance comes unique perspectives on failure, most often linked to fear. The way in which failure is perceived plays a significant role in the action-oriented characteristic of successful entrepreneurs. Brian Takeda, owner of *muzi tea bar*, calls failure the "lesson-fee" for doing business: "I haven't seen a failure," he says. "Everything was a learning, and so I see learning as the cost of doing business."

The lesson-fee perspective is clearly linked to the "failure as a blessing" philosophy, which many entrepreneurs talked about extensively. Brewmaster owner, Terry Smith, says that while we can't see the good in the failure at the time it happens, years later we see the lesson-fee that allowed us to become the person we were meant to be. Terry remembers, as a young man, feeling devastated because he didn't get a position he desperately wanted with a pulpmill company. A few years later, after having gone back to university to further his training in chemistry and biochemistry, he got a much better job selling high-tech medical equipment. Eventually, he was able to see the opportunity afforded by this "disaster".

Several of the entrepreneurs had lost jobs or were fired, and only then, did they use their talents and skills to create a business. Laura Prosko, of Prosko Group Productions Inc., was dismayed by the loss of her job as a marketing agent for a radio station.

Without such adversity, she wouldn't have started her own event management company, which now has her accepting government contracts for political events. And she probably wouldn't have experienced the thrill of being a stand-up comedian, nor organized stand-up comedy shows at the famous Sylvia Hotel on English Bay, Vancouver. Sometimes, the loss of a job frees us up to do what we were meant to do.

Not all of the entrepreneurs went from a job to successful businesses. Some had first businesses that failed. Wally Garrick, of All Weather Shelters, owned a fish and tackle store that generated sales of over two million in its first year, but went bankrupt in less than 24 months due to errors made in inventory controls. He went through ten years of depression, struggling with guilt, inadequacy and insurmountable debt. Like others in debt and despair, Wally began drinking and succumbed to alcoholism. As he told me of these times, his voice quivering and eyes swelling with tears, I remembered the well-repeated statistic that eighty percent of all businesses would fail in the first two years. But I rarely heard about those business owners who recovered by starting anew. These stories of "finding a way back" are often the stories entrepreneurs need to be reminded of, particularly during their darkest hours.

After winning the war against alcohol, Wally set out to clearly define what he wanted and didn't want in his ideal business. One of his personal criteria was to run a business that had the controls and systems which would ensure his previous mistakes in the "Ma and Pa" operation would not be repeated. Because his credit was poor, he needed to open a business that would initially require little or no inventory, hence his choice of building outdoor mobile shelters. The materials for these shelters could be purchased after customer down payments had been made. Immediately after placing a few advertisements for his product, Wally had twelve orders. Today, All Weather Shelters is one of the top Canadian manufacturers and distributors of outdoor shelters for oil and gas companies.

Wally and his wife Dawn recently sold their business and have purchased several acres of land in a fishing community along the shores of Lesser Slave Lake in northern Alberta. They built cabins that are rented to avid fisherman, and are proud to employ locals who built the cabins and run a restaurant. Wally now gets to fish daily and hear fish stories, just as he did in his first business. Things have come full circle, as his ability to overcome fear and depression has led him to the life he truly desired.

Recognizing Gifts

Consider the blessings of seven-time Tour de France winner, Lance Armstrong, who believes being diagnosed with advanced testicular cancer was both the best and worst day of his life. Today, Armstrong is one of the leading figures in the fight against cancer, using his gifts to make a far greater difference to humanity than his winnings as a cyclist.

Such gifts are abundant in the business world as well. Many entrepreneurs shared stories of coming back from the brink of financial disaster, carrying with them this wisdom: the blessing often arrives shortly after the lowest point. This may seem obvious or trite to some entrepreneurs, yet when faced with possible business failure, many never see the "silver lining".

When recalling year-one of his business, Just One Drop Water Shops owner, Darren McDowell, spoke with great emotion about the point at which he was about to close his doors. A father at nineteen, Darren had always assumed responsibility for his family, and now, two decades later, was facing the very real possibility of putting his family into financial ruin. Eyes down and face flushed, he told me of the day he reluctantly agreed with a mentor to give his business a few more weeks to turn a profit. The next day, the phone started ringing. And never stopped. Two years later, Darren was awarded the Surrey Chamber of Commerce Entrepreneur of the Year.

Trent Dyrsmid, in six-figure debt after running his business for a year, showed unusual perspective by repeatedly acknowledging that the "tipping point"—the point at which the business would turn a profit—would soon arrive. He saw continual improvement in sales, and the possibility of going back to a job to pay off debt was unthinkable. Yet, when meeting with his investor to request more money, Trent was asked a challenging question: "Don't you think you should just shut it down?" Refusing to buckle under financial strain, Trent remained adamant that the tipping point would soon arrive. He convinced the investor to keep the business going just a little longer, and the following month Dyrand Systems broke even.

Consider This

▶ During and after difficult situations, write down the gift you received from that experience. It may be a new relationship with yourself or others. It may be new insights into developing systems. It may be the strengthening of a necessary skill or attitude. Like The Phoenix, rise from the ashes with the gift that is life-giving. As Wally Garrick advises, don't let it take you ten years to start living again.

Tapping into Spiritual Beliefs

For some entrepreneurs, the fear of financial failure was mitigated by a spiritual belief. Mike Robinson, co-owner of Ultra Span Structures, experienced times when he didn't know where his next meal was coming from or how he'd support his family of four. Yet, he and his wife Suzanne had a strong belief they would be looked after. A neighbour would stop by with a few extra loaves of bread. The phone would ring with a new contract. In the first years of his business, Mike remembers these times as being emotionally difficult, and certainly wouldn't want to go through them again, yet has learned to deal with and accept risk, knowing a Higher Power is at work.

One entrepreneur interviewed was earning over two hundred dollars per hour in his accounting business when he left it behind, pursuing his vision of becoming a top speaker with the purpose of helping the world's poor. Because Azim Jamal has family to support, I asked whether he viewed this career change as a substantial risk. He replied calmly that although family and friends doubted the wisdom of his decision, he knew it was his calling to use his God-given talents to make a difference. Because of this strong sense, his perspective on risk is that it is non-existent. This became apparent to all early on in Azim's new career, as he gave over 200 keynote speeches in a year and wrote his first book, 7 *Steps to Lasting Happiness*. Azim's advice to entrepreneurs: "When you find your calling and believe in yourself, nothing, not even financial risk, will lessen your desire to reach your dreams."

Again and again, I listened to stories of coming back from the brink, both financially and personally. I can only conclude what is implied by these experiences: that we are given what we need when we need it, and secondly, that our commitment will be tested over and over again. This does not mean that we will never fail these tests, but that the tests are designed to reveal *The David* within. And those that endure the tests know one thing for certain: too many people give up too soon— emotionally, mentally, financially. They give up just before the tipping point arrives.

Consider This

▶ Of all the conversations that centered on action, entrepreneurs advised follow-through and commitment more than anything else; having the discipline to act daily, doing what you say you will do, and seeing it through to the end rather than following every whim or being held hostage by every distraction. This doesn't mean you should never change course—we all have to do that in order to adapt effectively to change—but in order to have true belief in ourselves, in order to come to terms with risk and failure, seeing an idea through to its conception is crucial, whether it be a single personal goal or a five-year company vision.

▶ Eric Huang advises entrepreneurs to take calculated risks in any business venture, but, "Once you take the risk, put all your heart and all your ability into it, and never have a doubt it's going to work." Are you willing to do what it takes? Do your actions demonstrate that you're willing?

▶ Keep a log of your actions for one week every month to see if they show a clear commitment. Ask yourself, "Would I hire myself to do this work?" If the answer is no, reflect on what you need to be doing to demonstrate that commitment.

Stretching Comfort Zones

To lessen fears, several entrepreneurs suggested challenging comfort zones outside of your business first. By doing this, you develop more confidence to act despite fear in any area of life. Darren McDowell overcame his fear of heights by parachuting. His personal power that came from doing this helped him confidently build his first business. Laura Prosko purposely set out to challenge her comfort zone while building her business by doing stand-up comedy. Today, she is so successful with her acts that she's earned the status of one of the top eight comedians in British Columbia, with big businesses calling her up to do gigs.

Patti Fasan was deathly afraid of public speaking, yet needed to develop this skill if she was to rise to the top of her dream profession as a consultant in the ceramic tile industry. She attended a variety of seminars, and spoke to anyone who was willing to listen. She remembers her first presentation in New York City, where she was so nervous, she memorized an entire two-and-a-half-hour speech! Eventually, she became comfortable enough to share her professional expertise with companies around the world.

Eleanor Roosevelt said, "You must do the thing you think you cannot do." We often forget that the "Courage Muscle" activated in personal matters is the same used in business matters.

Studying the Numbers

When making decisions involving large financial risk, thorough research is essential and often reduces fear of failure. Some entrepreneurs felt their business risk was fairly low because they or their partners were exceptional number-crunchers and problem-solvers. Fundraising guru Harvey McKinnon, who admitted winning great sums of money playing poker in high school and university, says that understanding the odds cuts down on risk. Similarly, Brian Takeda, while planning the *muzi tea bar* concept as a university project with Mars Koo, recognized Mars' exceptional research and number crunching talents. Brian admits that without Mars, the company would have endured many more financial hardships. Today, Mars continues to be the litmus test for many decisions made at their popular and trendy tea bars.

There are other entrepreneurs who are adamant that intuition be used prior to number crunching. John Stanton, owner and president of the Running Room, says that he uses intuition in site location, validating it with fact afterwards. "If I'm looking at a new area, I'll go in and run around, drive around, have a look at the area and say, 'Yes, this makes sense for the Running Room.' Then I validate it with some demographics and logistics, but we never choose a location based on just demographics or numbers." John's experience is common among most business owners, with intuition being the single most talked-about factor in decision-making and risk.

Wisdom in Action

Progress always involves risk. You can't steal second base and keep your foot on first.

Frederick B. Wilcox

Do not stop thinking of life as an adventure. You have no security unless you can live bravely, excitedly, imaginatively, unless you choose a challenge instead of a competence.

Eleanor Roosevelt

Write down three points of action you will take after reviewing this chapter. Then reflect on the quotes above and how these words translate to action in your life.

Chapter Four

Intuition in the Face of Fear

Trusting God, your "gut", your "guide", "the universe". These are some ways entrepreneurs described intuition, adding that they regretted times they didn't listen to it. Fundraising expert, Harvey McKinnon, tells of a time when he was on a board that was about to finalize a decision to hire someone. His intuition screamed, "NO", although the person interviewed well and had all the talents, skills and awards of a dream applicant. She was hired, but four months later, his inner knowing proved right, as discoveries about her lack of integrity and honesty were revealed.

Many other entrepreneurs told stories of not listening to their intuition. As a pioneer of the majestic Clydesdale show, Canadian Clyde Ride owner, Wendee Lynn Cristante, had little information from which to make business decisions, and those people who could have helped were the, "Hush-hush old boys' club." She notes, "My whole business has been trial and error and I can list hundreds of situations along the way where I have felt very uncomfortable about decisions that I was making. Now I am in tune with when I feel that way. There's a reason for it, and I really need to take a look at it."

Sound familiar? We are creatures who like to think predominately with our heads rather than our whole selves, but when the body, or "gut" is not in harmony with the head, look out! This, perhaps, is the hardest lesson to grasp early on in entrepreneurial ventures, but can be learned by all. To release the fear and let the intuition flow, entrepreneurs suggested:

▶ Clarifying and Committing to What Matters

▶ Becoming Quiet

▶ Tapping into Your Five Senses

▶ Using Experience as a Guide

▶ Observing Body Language when Hiring

Clarifying and Committing to What Matters

Kathy Kolbe, author of *Powered by Instinct: 5 Rules for Trusting Your Guts*, warns her readers of what they risk by not confirming what matters most in life. "You're either willing to act with a sense of purpose or you're not. If you play around with the prescriptions for committing to very little, you'll be sending a message to yourself that you haven't made a decision to trust your guts." Committing to your business involves taking time to get clear about what it is that you most want and why.

Azim Jamal spiritually connects this commitment and clarity to intuition as well, saying, "We are all guided by our Creator, but if we don't know where we're going, how are we going to be guided there?" This is seen in the planning stages of many businesses. Brewmasters owner and commercial landlord, Terry Smith, says that most tenancy applications he gets do not demonstrate in-depth research. Sketchy business plans include few strategies for surviving the first six to twelve months with little or no cash flow. When research is complete, Terry stresses, entrepreneurs need to know that they are entering a long-term commitment where there can be no waffling, no shaky commitment. That's where self-awareness, or an understanding of our passions, motivators, and patterns of thinking, can provide us with the foundation for commitment. When the research on the business and self is thorough, the likelihood of true commitment to the business and an entrepreneurial life is much higher.

Becoming Quiet

While some entrepreneurs say they're too busy to hear intuition which guides others, many purposely set aside time to connect with that calm, inner knowing. Marketing expert, Wendy McClelland, explains, "We've become so bombarded by so many messages, that for a lot of us, our intuition is very quiet these days. And so to get back to that, spend some time alone. No distractions: no TV, no radio, no cell phone, no people. Go out in the wilderness if you have to. Sit in a quiet room. Start to focus on one thing in your life. Whether it be a relationship you're struggling with, a health issue or a business problem, try to stay focused on that problem and allow your mind to start giving you some feedback."

Beginning entrepreneurs may be tempted to skip the quiet time that fosters self-growth, yet for people like Ted Cawkwell, this time is integral to effective decision-making. When Ted undertook a huge financial risk by purchasing raw land to build Milton Lake Lodge, a luxurious fishing resort, intuition combined with meditation was crucial to his success. He learned to be still despite huge risks and working around the clock. "I did so many things right in such a short time with this business. How could I have been just 'lucky'? I know I didn't have enough knowledge to make that many decisions correctly. I was also tired and worn out going in 100 different directions, but my intuition somehow guided me through this and I did a lot of things right because of it."

In one of his memorable talks, human potential expert, Wayne Dyer, said that when we are consumed with worry or fear, we show disbelief in God. This also holds true for those of us who feel uncomfortable being still. There is often an urge to control, to be doing something "useful". Yet, the more I learn about intuition, the more I believe it whispers or shouts the guidance we need at the time we need it—we just need to be still enough to hear it. Carving time to "do nothing" and trusting that it will result in "something", is a belief in something greater than us—a loving and nurturing force.

Tapping into Your Five Senses

Faced with indecision and fretting over possible consequences, I asked Executive Coach, Mary Ellen Sanajko, what I should do. She guided me through an exercise that tapped into my intuition in a sensory way, where my body felt the answer. By having me go inside to the quiet, knowing centre of my Self, and then visualizing the colours and textures of this place of knowing, Mary Ellen helped me connect to my intuition and feel confident that I had made the right choice.

Graciously, Mary Ellen agreed to share this process so that you may benefit too:

Take some deep breaths, filling your stomach as you breathe in, and exhaling as your stomach flattens. Breathe in relaxation. Each time you blow out, allow yourself to relax. Do this three times. It may be easier if you close your eyes.

Notice how you're feeling. What's going on inside you?

As you're inside, go to that place inside you that knows things … that place where your intuition makes itself known. Breathe into that place and put your hand there.

Where is it? In your tummy? Your chest? Just notice. What's the temperature? If it had a colour, what colour would it be? What's your sense of the size of this place? How big is it? How dense is it? Connect to that place, and notice what it's like now that you've gotten to know it a bit better, and know that you can return there anytime you want.

Come back to the present.

Using Experience as a Guide

I believe that fully accessing intuition can lead us to good decisions. I also believe in the value of experience; the value of the lesson-fee. Farah Perelmuter says that intuition and experience go hand in hand. As you experience certain situations, you are better able to combine intuition with this experience to make decisions. She notes, for instance, that she has stronger intuitive guidance in marketing, which is her specialty area, in comparison to her husband, whose forte is selling. Similarly, Elana Rosenfeld of Kicking Horse Coffee says, "When you've been faced with certain situations or asked certain questions in the past, you have a better idea of what decisions to make, particularly if your gut is clearly in alignment with that decision." Ideally, entrepreneurs combine experience, research and intuition to lessen risk and fears in making major decisions. But, when neither experience nor research is available, intuition is a good place to start.

Similar to sharpening intuition through experience, travel is also highlighted as a way of developing intuition. Sandra Sereda owns and operates diverse businesses, largely due to the extensive traveling she's done. Sandra advises, "Be aware of all the trends. You can get caught up in the four corners of where you live, your own little world, but being global, reading and traveling, can help you discover where things are going." She notes that her constant attention to detail in other businesses around the world has sharpened her intuition when it comes to sensing what customers want and are willing to pay for.

Consider This

▶ What helps you connect to your intuition? How does it make itself known to you?

▶ Are you observing other businesses and reflecting on experiences in your business? Are you gifting

yourself with solitude or time in nature? What
other steps could you take to strengthen intuition?

Observing Body
Language when Hiring

To hire the best people, entrepreneurs combined information
from group and individual interviews with personal intuition.
Even this comprehensive strategy is not foolproof, according to
Trent Dyrsmid. Many people approach him with powerful
resumes and interview exceptionally well, but after being hired,
show their true colours. Despite this common problem,
entrepreneurs can increase the chances of choosing the right
person for the job and company.

**Picking up on non-verbal clues is key in confirming gut
feelings.** Police officers, detectives, and undercover government
agents are trained to detect these clues. Some of the more
obvious clues that often indicate nervousness or uncom-
fortableness are scratching or rubbing the neck and face, crossing
legs or folding arms, and pointing feet away from the person
talking. Subtle facial expressions are often fleeting, but when
noticed, can give you valuable insight. Shifting eyes, exaggerated
movement of eyebrows and dilating pupils, may suggest some
hidden emotion or concealing of fact. The more proficient you
are in this detection, the more likely it is your observation and
intuition will be aligned.

The significance of verbal and non-verbal clues can be seen
in Malcolm Gladwell's bestseller, *Blink: The Power of Thinking
Without Thinking*. Gladwell interviews John Gottman, a well-
known researcher, who predicts, with alarming accuracy, the
success rate of marriages based on only one meeting. Gottman
does this by documenting and analyzing the largely non-verbal
clues couples give away while in conversation. During his
research, he discovered that when individuals or couples talk
about themselves or their relationships, they are neither objective
nor particularly accurate. Rather than tell couples to describe
their marriage, Gottman asked them to discuss something

involving their marriage, like children or pets. Entrepreneurs who interview can also minimize questions involving self-description, focusing instead on previous jobs held or past experiences involving solutions and emotional responses. This type of probing is likely to result in a more complete picture of the prospective employee.

In some cultures, it is not uncommon for prospective employees to be invited to play a round of golf or other sport, with the executive's goal being to observe the way interviewees handle themselves. These observations lead to conclusions about values, attitudes, and perspectives. Executives can then see more clearly whether these individuals would be a good fit for their companies. Often, the non-verbal clues people give off are as telling as any verbal evidence.

Consider This

▶ Engage in a sport with other business owners and practice picking up non-verbal clues that help you decide whether or not to pursue a relationship with them. Write down all the clues after the game and analyze them according to what recent research (and your intuition) says about these clues. For example, how does the individual react to a poorly executed shot? How does he or she maintain rapport when not talking? What facial expressions and gestures are used when others play well or poorly?

▶ One excellent resource to assist you in recognizing and adopting positive clues is Leil Lowndes' *How to Talk to Anyone: 92 Little Tricks for Big Success in Relationships.* Consider Lowndes' humorous advice not only for using intuition in interviewing, but also for creating favorable impressions: "Even before your lips part and the first syllable escapes, the essence of YOU has already axed its way into their brains. The way you look and the way you move is more than eighty percent of someone's first impression of you. Not one word need be spoken."

▶ Marketing expert Wendy McClelland suggests journaling to record and reflect on your intuition. She says if you're not sure whether to trust your intuition, write down the situation and your gut feeling about the person or experience. Read this one month later to see if your intuition was right and what might have happened if you had followed a different path.

Wisdom in Action

"When so much of your life is unstable—you haven't got a regular income, you're dealing with new people, you're operating a new business, you're trying to learn new expertise—that's a whole lot of instability. So intuition can provide you with a sense of stability because it's your way of saying, 'There's something helping me.' "

Mike Robinson, Ultra Span Structures

One of the reasons so few of us act, instead of react, is because we are continually stifling our deepest impulses.

Henry Miller

Write down three points of action you will take after reviewing this chapter. Then reflect on the quotes above and how these words translate to action in your life.

Part Two

The Awareness Principle: Seeing *The David* in Business, in Self

The universe is full of magical things patiently waiting for
our wits to grow sharper.

Bertrand Russell

Chapter Five

What Matters? Clarifying and Committing to Values

In the past decade of self-development literature, experts continually swear by the value of having a mission, vision, and goals. They say all successful people create and continually revisit them with passion and conviction. Curious to see if this statement was true for the entrepreneurs I spoke with, I listened carefully to their discussion of future endeavors, their hopes and dreams and other things they held near their heart. What I heard both affirmed my own research and experience and challenged the common wisdom of business and self-development books.

In over 100 hours of conversations with leading business owners, the theme of clarifying and living by a set of values was consistently emphasized. In fact, several entrepreneurs, when asked what sets them apart from the competition, said they lived by their values, with honesty and integrity being at the top of the list. Doing what we say we will do seems so obvious, doesn't it? Yet many people do not operate this way. These entrepreneurs do, and have shared insights that, among other things, can

strengthen one of the most important pillars of your business—
client trust. They include:

▶ Committing to Integrity

▶ Defining Success

▶ Zooming In, Zooming Out

▶ Embracing Spiritual Values

▶ Hiring Values

▶ Carving Time

▶ Coming to Grips with "Less Is More"

Committing to Integrity

Trent Dyrsmid lives his life in integrity. He told me of his
unsuccessful attempt to build his first business, as an e-
commerce service provider. When the company failed in its early
stages, Trent shut it down and immediately returned all $50,000
owing to his investor, although the investor wasn't expecting
the money to be returned. "I always thought about maintaining
my integrity as a credible person by never taking more than
what was mine to take, and always making sure that I made a
deposit back into the 'relationship bank account' because I always
saw the bigger picture."

Integrity is also crucial to entrepreneurs because they are
inundated with requests to take part in various ventures, whether they be for profit or not. Tami Reilly, president of GO Get
Organized, says her success has largely been influenced by
staying aligned with her core beliefs: "I've walked away from
quote-unquote 'opportunities', because they weren't within my
integrity comfort zone." Similarly, Peter Legge of Canada Wide
Magazines and Communications, says, "We are asked to do a
lot of crazy things here, but I just won't do them. Our reputation
is way too important."

John Stanton of the Running Room says he is constantly
turning down requests from companies hoping to place ads in
his monthly magazine. John explains that these companies violate

what he considers to be "family values", giving the example of a running magazine that readily places ads for Viagra. Taking his company decisions through a three-way test helps him also ensure that values are considered first and foremost. "We want a win for the customer, a win for the Running Room, and we want to make sure there's a win for the community." When decisions are made like this, there is a sense of stability, clarity, and assurance that the company is built on the strength of its values.

Defining Success

One way to clarify values is to define true success. I asked business owners whether their definition of success changed over the years. The great majority responded by saying that success now encompasses more areas of life, with greater appreciation and attention being paid to relationships, family and health. **While there is much debate on what constitutes balance, the entrepreneurs I interviewed generally agreed it is the peace and well-being that comes from paying attention to what really matters in life**.

Ken Funk, former president of Golden Valley Foods says: "I dedicated my life to building a business. And my family was important to me and remains important, but they would very often get put on the back burner because you justify things by saying, 'Well, I'm really doing it for my family too.' Today, I would say that my definition of success is quite different. I think if you can achieve and maintain both in your professional and private life, a balance, whatever that means—balance is different things to different people—I think that's success. The things that are important to me today are my family and my friends and my health. Business would be third or fourth in my priorities. It doesn't mean that I'm not dedicated or committed to the business, but it doesn't take up all of my waking hours and all of my focus."

Like Ken, some entrepreneurs told of notions of success changing from earning the big bucks to the ability to enjoy life and live it fully. Friends once asked Rob McGregor if he collects anything, and he surprised them by saying, "Experiences." Rob explained to me that "There are so many possibilities for experiences in this world. It's the most readily available commodity and really doesn't cost anything. So success is that openness to the awareness of the possibilities around us." Alphonse Seward agrees. "The real definition of success for me now is when a day is really full and it has moments of joy and sorrow and the whole gamut. That's a rich day."

▶ **My Story**

I remember one rich day, a day where I felt I had done it all. A day where I felt *The David* within. It wasn't filled with extraordinary experiences, but one that involved making a difference in the lives of others. In the morning I gave a seminar to a group in Regina, and then had a long drive back home with my two children. I had achieved my purpose in helping people commit to what they most wanted in their lives, but was anxious to get home. My children noticed a beautiful European-style castle with a Miniature Land sign, and begged to go in. As I sped by, ignoring their pleas, something inside me told me to stop. I turned the car around and drove into the amusement site, much to my children's delight. As we paid our ticket fees and opened the door to see the miniatures, I was astounded by all the beautiful creations, the owner, an elderly Austrian man, had made. When we left, I thought about what a rich day it had been, and how I almost said "no" to this richness, this opportunity to connect with my sons in a world of imagination. The words of speaker Linda Edgecombe come to mind whenever I hesitate to have more experiences: "When is the last time you did something for the first time?"

When I spoke to Rob McGregor and Alphonse Seward, I was struck by their gentle and peaceful nature. I believe, that at least part of this attribute, stems from their determination to live a life of harmony and balance. Executive Performance Coach,

Peri Shawn, also exemplifies this by giving herself what she needs to be a whole person. This in turn is beneficial for her clients. "We are only as good to others as we've been to ourselves. If I don't take care of me, then I can't be effective or helpful to others. Most people don't have time to think; most don't have time to take care of their health. So I have a responsibility to ensure that I keep that balance."

Consider This

▶ Some entrepreneurs have always had the same definition of success. Brian Scudamore says that he has always wanted just one thing: to be happy. He feels successful because he is passionate about 1-800-GOT-JUNK? and looks forward to work every morning. His happiness also involves going for walks along the beach with his toddler and taking a couple of hours a week to play squash with friends. This definition is much the same as John Stanton's, who says success is not knowing whether he's working or playing. "If somebody asked me how many days a year I work, I probably work 360. But if you asked me how many days a year I play, I'd say 360 because the majority of the time, I'm doing things I'm passionately embraced with." Notice both John and Brian's definitions emphasize a sense of wholeness and balance. Does your definition of success include your whole self or only one aspect of self? What would it mean to have a more whole definition?

▶ Like Brian, John, and many other successful entrepreneurs, your definition of success can be simple. In fact, the simpler it is, the easier you can regularly measure and track that success.

Zooming In, Zooming Out

Another method of defining core values is "zooming out" to write your own eulogy. Examine what you would want said about you at your funeral. I facilitated a group which had explored a number of activities to identify core values, but when they wrote the eulogy, one woman approached me, saying, "What I see as values in this eulogy are quite different from the ones I've listed for other activities." It was then I realized people often focus on one aspect of success, forgetting to examine other, more crucial, elements. While it's important to have focused income goals and business growth, adopting a wide-angle-lens look at life can help provide balance.

Without asking entrepreneurs to discuss the end of their life, some did when referring to their life's purpose. Tami Reilly said, "The thing I want to have on my tombstone, what I want to be most remembered for when I'm dead, is that I was a good friend and a good mom, and that I gave more than I took." Although Tami has many business ambitions, she doesn't list these on her tombstone. Rob McGregor laughed as he told me of visualizing himself on his deathbed, smiling and saying, "Ya, it was a good life."

Another daily check to clarify values, involves "zooming in" to focus on the significance of daily events. Ask yourself "What do I remember most about today?" Notice whether these memories involve particular people, whether they are positive or negative, or whether they are connected to certain events or roles in your life (ie: parenting, business, spirituality, health, finances, recreation). This exercise reveals much of what you truly consider "important" on a daily basis. Tami Reilly illustrates her revelation when she was sitting in her son Max's room, watching him build Lego.

"And what were we really doing? Not anything. He was putting together some Lego and we were talking about the different types of Lego and he was thinking about how to build the pieces. From that day, that's what I remember most. And probably a lot of other things happened that day, but that's what I recall most specifically. And so if we're all here to learn, I guess I'm really trying to learn about the little things, with not so much success or failure tied into the big things."

Consider This

▶ At the end of a day, what do you remember most? Is it a little thing or a BIG thing? What was valuable about these memories? How does this value impact your actions in business? In other areas of life?

▶ When I facilitate seminars about committing to what matters in life, I ask participants to do a series of activities to help uncover their values. I then ask them to write these values down in order of importance. Most people have great difficulty doing this because they've never taken time to really define their values and the importance they place on these values. Once they have their values in order, I ask them to estimate how much time they want to spend doing things that encompass these values and compare that to actual time spent. Try doing this for a week. Almost always, people are surprised by how little time they spend in certain areas of their life they believe to be valuable.

Embracing Spiritual Values

Many entrepreneurs emphasized values that are connected to their spiritual beliefs. Whether their belief is rooted in religion or not, most of the entrepreneurs carry strong convictions about the role of spiritual laws in their personal and professional lives. Peter Legge refers to the Bible's "You reap what you sow," while

others talked of Buddhist beliefs like Karma, or "What goes
around comes around." Trent Dyrsmid explains:

> "Everything you do is the equivalent of sending out a
> bolt of energy. So, if you're sending out positive energy
> it will circle around and come back to you. If you're
> sending out negative energy, it will circle around and
> come back to you. I think of that constantly as I'm doing
> business with people and I'm talking with people and as
> I'm conducting myself as an entrepreneur and as a
> person. Think: 'Is this how I want to be treated? Is this
> the reputation that I want to create for myself? Is this a
> person whose respect I want to have not just this week,
> but next year, next decade?' "

The reap-what-is-sown belief is exemplified in many entrepreneurial stories. Jewelry designer, Susan Rind, was showing a
new line in New York when she noticed a couple admiring the
home décor she displayed. At this particular show, buyers were
the only people allowed to enter the rooms of designers, yet
Susan welcomed them in. Timidly, the couple asked Susan if
she would consider submitting her home décor ideas to a "how
to" publication. When she graciously accepted, they were taken
aback by her willingness to help, saying, "Most artists don't want
to share their secrets." Susan's kind and generous nature resulted
in several of her creations being featured on the cover of a coffee
table hardcover book, along with a chapter dedicated to her
unique designs. This led to the giant craft chain Michael's, using
Susan's wirework ideas on utensils in their 528-page "how to"
book. Susan reflects, "It was a nice domino effect of allowing
those people to come into my room that day."

Recently, Susan extended another "random act of kindness" to
thirty-five women in an evening tribute to her mentor, Ella Little.
Gorgeous dragonfly pins made from Swarovski Crystal and sterling silver were given away with a reminder to pass on the kindness whenever they looked at or thought about their pins. This
not only resulted in Susan receiving more business, but also,
and perhaps, more importantly, left a group of women feeling
connected and aware of their potential impact on humanity.

If the sowing-what-we-reap belief reminds us to be kind to others, so too does the belief that we're all connected in some way. Elana Rosenfeld saw Kicking Horse Coffee as a vehicle for educating the public on health and environmental concerns associated with the use of pesticides in growing coffee. Elana wants to not only make a difference in the health of her customers, but also in the health of her suppliers and Mother Earth. At the Canadian Living Lakes Conference in 2004, Elana said, "Many people think that the sole reason to consume organic coffee is for their own health benefit. More importantly, the reason you should drink organic coffee is to protect the water table of the growing regions and the women and children that hand-pick the coffee cherries." Feeling the connectedness to people and the environment is becoming more and more prevalent in the world of business, as entrepreneurs develop increasing global awareness and a desire to positively impact the world around them.

Ted Cawkwell's connectedness comes from regularly sending out good intentions for the people that come to his lodge. During the construction of the lodge, Ted meditated daily, sending intentions that it be a place where people feel at peace, have fun, and get back to the essence of themselves. Some may call this the power of prayer; others refer to it as connecting with their spiritual guide or the universe. Many entrepreneurs are becoming more spiritual in nature, recognizing that their own hard work, when assisted by the Divine, produces results they never thought possible. Ted repeatedly told me of his belief that there were forces at work helping him oversee the construction of his upscale fishing lodge, built and filled with customers in a single year.

Mike Robinson, of Ultra Span Structures, is the district governor for Toastmasters in British Columbia, a volunteer position that sometimes exceeds the average workweek. When I asked him why he had taken this position on, as it is not a source of potential referrals for his business, he said, "All human thought, all human essence, if you like, is connected." He explains this by referring to the work of biologist Rupert

Sheldrake, whose research into collective memory suggests that what we learn as human beings is influenced by all those who have learned it before.

One part of Sheldrake's research involved a London newspaper, *The Evening Standard*, which supplied its test crossword puzzle in advance of being published, so that several groups could complete it the day before publication, and other groups the day after publication. The groups also completed a control crossword, which was not published during that time, measuring each individual's ability to do that type of puzzle. The students who were in the group that completed the crossword after its publication performed twenty-five percent better than the students who completed it prior to publication. This research has been validated by many other studies as well, and seems to suggest that the energy that exists in thought directly impacts those around it. It makes sense, then, that entrepreneurs who purposely seek out successful business people will both consciously learn from their mentors, and be influenced by the energy of their thought. In turn, this gift can be passed on to others.

Hiring Values

Several of the entrepreneurs talked about the importance of a values-fit within their organization, particularly when interviewing prospective employees. Brian Scudamore says that he is slow to hire, as he wants to be sure people hired are an appropriate fit for his company, culturally (energetic, fun, passionate) and in values. His company is built around four values that form the acronym PIPE: Passion, Integrity, Professionalism and Empathy.

Happy to share information in a professional and passionate way, Brian is a great model of the company's values. He says that PIPE has helped his company keep on track with what matters most. Using the examples of appearance and communication, Brian doesn't enforce a dress code, but if someone arrives at work looking sloppy, he points out the value of professionalism, which needs to be adhered to. If managers deal harshly with a fellow employee, they are reminded of the value of empathy. Constantly referring back to values helps keep Brian's company focused on what matters most. With business growing exponentially (70 million in sales in 2005 with forecast sales of one billion by 2012), 1-800-GOT-JUNK? is a model for entrepreneurs seeking exponential growth while remaining true to core values.

Consider This

▶ Interview yourself, using questions that reveal values. Questions like: "Why did I make certain decisions in my life?" will help you recognize the values apparent in your answers. Are these the values you want employees to display as you build your company? How can you become a model of these values? Regularly take time to reflect on decisions you're making to see if they are aligned with your company values.

Carving Time

Some business books promise to reveal time management secrets that work every day, every time. I looked forward to hearing these secrets from entrepreneurs, but was surprised to discover that many struggled with using time effectively. Although to an outsider, these entrepreneurs make excellent use of their time, they admitted that time, or lack of it, was a constant battle. Here are some nuggets of wisdom that may help you develop a system that works for you.

Azim Jamal once owned his own accounting business and put his knowledge of numbers to good use. He systematized his time by creating a budget for the week, which maps out his number of hours used for sleep, health, meditation, community service, and business activities like reading, writing, creating products, branding, and website fine-tuning. He also allows for seventeen hours of "flex time", which he says is important because there are things that come up over the course of the week that will take precedence over his schedule. He gives an example of his teenage daughter asking to talk about an issue that arose in her personal life: "If she wants to talk to me and I'm in my schedule, I'll drop my schedule and go with my daughter because she's important to me. So the flex time allows you to go with the flow and not miss the opportunities."

Azim periodically adds up the total hours spent in a week under each category and compares it to his goal. He then reflects on what he's learned from this variance, and journals about his life-learnings from the week's events. Azim says the discipline of systematizing his use of time and then reflecting on it has been one of the most important ingredients to his success as a speaker, writer and philanthropist. Perhaps most importantly, it impacts whether or not he is aligned with his life-vision. In *Life Balance is a Choice*, co-authored with Nido Qubein, Azim says whatever is important in life is often not seen as urgent, and so people don't do it. But with his time budget, Azim considers all important aspects of life so that he remains healthy physically, emotionally, mentally and spiritually. He is committed to going out twice a week with his wife, picking his kids up from school and coaching his son in soccer. Even on the drive to school, Azim teaches his kids to use their time well by saying morning prayers and memorizing inspiring quotes from the great sages in history.

A last, astounding note about Azim's system of time is that he goes to sleep around 8:30 pm weekdays and is up at around 1:00 am, refreshed and ready to work through the night. In this way, he has a few hours of uninterrupted time to plan, produce products, and meditate. While his isn't a schedule most people would entertain, it is certainly inspiring to those who want to have more hours in a day to get things done. For Azim, working in the early morning allows for creativity and balance: "When I'm in town, I drop my kids at school and I pick them up from school. I go to most of their activities and I love doing that. I make it up when I wake up at 1:00 am; everyone is sleeping, so

I'm not imposing on people's time and I get my forty-two to forty-five hours of sleep a week. That's enough for me."

Consider This

▶ Do a "Time Diary" for a minimum of one week and compare your time goals to the actual number of hours invested in important areas of your life.

▶ Reflect on what you can do to improve the variance. Consider waking up one hour earlier each morning and record the difference this small change makes in your overall balance and feelings of accomplishment.

▶ **My Story**

Following Azim's system for managing time, I discovered six areas to improve, either by committing more or less time to each area. A moment of awareness came as I looked at the variance of how I had spent my time versus what my ideal was. To my astonishment, I spent double the number of hours writing and responding to e-mail than I did in conversation with my husband. I also noticed that I spent considerably more time cleaning my house than I did playing with my children. These difficult insights brought about an immediate change in my use of time, and all because of a simple system, that when used diligently, is a significant tool in refining personal balance and renewing commitments to values.

Other Tips on Planning Your Time

Executive Performance Coach, Peri Shawn, reminds entrepreneurs that "time is our greatest gift", and using it in a way that expresses our highest values leads to a fulfilling life. Peri says her highest values are learning, family and spirituality. If something doesn't fit into one of these three categories, she won't do it.

Doing a daily plan at the same time every day can be very productive. Within this structure, Brian Scudamore lists the top three items on his daily "to do" list and consistently achieves this minimum goal. He then asks himself if there are other things on his list he can get rid of or shuffle around to make room for another, more pressing activity. Brian says that focusing on completion of these tasks prevents "overwhelm". "Rather than have 27 items on my list, I say, 'What are the three?' Let me get three done, and if I want to add three more, then great, but not allowing myself to be flooded with tasks."

When Terry Smith worked as a sales rep for a medical company, he began his day by doing his least favorite work first. While not every entrepreneur is in a position to do this, many people benefit from "getting it out of the way," having more enthusiasm for the remainder of the day. Since many people procrastinate to avoid doing those least favorite activities, accomplishing just three of the actions you typically resist before the mid-point in your workday, helps productivity.

Maureen Fitzgerald considers the morning hours of 9:00 am to noon to be her most productive time. During these hours, she avoids distractions, including phone calls and e-mail, focusing entirely on projects at hand. Meetings and correspondence by phone or computer are scheduled between the hours of three and five, a time when many business people are generally *less* focused and energetic. Being aware of your own peak performance times allows you to arrange and re-arrange tasks for optimum use of time.

Harvard professor and comedian Loretta Laroche jokes that statistically, nothing much happens in the way of productivity an hour before and two hours after lunch breaks, so why not take a nap and send your employees home? In many parts of the world, Laroche's comical advice is taken to heart, with businesses closing for three hours in the afternoon, when people go home, eat, and rest before returning to work. While this may not be possible for your business, the idea of resting and relaxing to regain focus and use time well, could increase the individual and collective achievement of goals, and result in a happier, more balanced team.

Coming to Grips with "Less is More"

Two women spoke of their growing wisdom about the Less Is More philosophy, after being in business for decades. Ella Little says, that at 73, she has slowed down and is more comfortable with less going on. She says, "I'm not feeling compelled to have a lot of busy-ness in my life anymore. I used to pack it all in, but I'm not doing it as much anymore. And that's okay." Ella gave the example of working twelve-hour days, six-days-a-week and then regularly having guests over for dinner on evenings and weekends. Sandra Sereda says she has learned to have less going on. She admits this is especially difficult for many entrepreneurial women, who often look after their home, family and business, and have a great desire to have a healthy balance of the three. She advises women in business to always examine what really matters in their lives and let go of the rest.

Choosing what not to do is part of the Less Is More philosophy. Jim Collins, in *Good to Great*, says that one of the main reasons the top companies he researched were effective was because they had a clear vision of what they wanted, and said no to everything else. As well as clarity of vision, I believe entrepreneurs also need a clarity of values and an awareness of what they are best at, so that they can more easily set boundaries and feel good about declining opportunities that don't fit within those boundaries.

Wendy McClelland, Peri Shawn, and Patti Fasan all spoke about the significance of boundaries in their lives. They noted that it is easy for entrepreneurs to allow customers or clients to be first not only in business, but in personal space and time. Wendy gives examples of clients who become irritated when she refuses to work weekends or late into the evening. Patti notes that some clients are frustrated by the fact that she doesn't carry a cell phone when she travels. "While it's important to be responsive," she explains, "we don't always have to be connected."

Consider This

▶ Whether you are a "Solopreneur" or employ a group of people, creating a system to manage your time better may help you achieve harmony and a personal sense of balance. Regularly evaluating this system and your progress within it is essential to taking your business and life to the next level.

Wisdom in Action

Harmony comes from clear priorities.

Jean Vanier

There are key turning points—points where we must take a stand and make deep personal commitments in order for change to take place. There is a peace that comes with the commitment to do what you really know is best, even though it's not easy or unopposed. But if we fail to take a stand, we get numbed into imbalance and disharmony, and by abdication, we become convinced that it's easier to live with the imbalance than to pay the price for balance.

Roger Merril, First Things First

Write down three points of action you will take after reviewing this chapter. Then reflect on the quotes above and how these words translate to action in your life.

Chapter Six

What Defines You?
Sculpting the One and Only

While awareness of our values and corresponding actions is growing with much self-development literature, so too is the idea that we, as individuals, are unique, and that tapping into this uniqueness is necessary to grow our business and keep ourselves and employees challenged and motivated. The results of this trend can be seen by looking back in history at gifted children like Einstein and Edison, who, despite significant challenges, went on to become highly successful in their fields. Michele Borba, author of *Parents Do Make A Difference,* says researchers, Victor and Mildred Goertzel, studied the lives of hundreds of creatively gifted and talented people in our century, and discovered that over three-fourths had tremendous handicaps, yet there was one common factor that helped them overcome challenges and become highly successful: they each had an individual in their lives who helped recognize and encourage a hidden talent. The development of this talent changed the world forever.

Entrepreneurs who talked about recognizing and maximizing their talents advised others to consider the following business-building actions:

▶ Focus on Strengths

▶ Define Dollars and Differences

▶ Know Your Uniqueness in Weakness

▶ Bring Out the Best in Others

Focus on Strengths

Today, more and more people are becoming aware of their own untapped potential, focusing on and developing talents that make them unique. On a company level, this same idea is emphasized through Jim Collins' groundbreaking business book, *Good to Great*. Jim and his team researched many top companies and found that the great majority of those companies were asking a question that others weren't: What can we be the best at? Not what can we be good at, but what can we do better than anyone else in the world? This question is important, not only for large companies, but also for small-business owners and prospective entrepreneurs, because clarity and focus comes from continually reflecting on this question. Speaker, Azim Jamal, agrees: "It's easy to differentiate between worst and best, but it's hard to see between good and best." He compares his two-decade accounting career, which he was very good at, to his work as a speaker, which he does better than anything else.

Going from good to best may involve years of self-reflection, just as it did for Azim, who found his "bestness" later in life. For beginning entrepreneurs, this self-reflection needs to show up in the form of a USP (Unique Selling Proposition). When I first heard of this from small-business expert Frances McGuckin, I was beginning to speak and write as an info-preneur, but didn't really think about how my services, products and talents were special or unique. In today's fiercely competitive business environment, it was something I had to develop. Rob McGregor of Spirit West Management, says that he and his partner, Lorraine Reiger, "spend a lot of time figuring out what it is that we are actually offering people ... why a person would choose us as opposed to someone else. If you can't articulate that, then you're in trouble. You're just one of many."

Maureen Wilson of Sweat Co., knows her USP revolves around her business as a "second home" for fitness enthusiasts. When asked what makes her gym different from hundreds of others in the heart of Vancouver, she says,

"I try to stay true to the style that we are at Sweat Co. So if a guy comes in and says, 'Where's your power cages?', he's going to know that this isn't really the culture for him. I keep trying to be true to that, to the quality we're offering, the care that we have for people. We need to care for our clients. We want them to feel at home when they're here. And I feel that if I keep moving towards that, as our specialty here, then people will come."

Similarly, the Running Room has a welcoming atmosphere, distinguishing it from many Big Box athletic stores. Over the past two decades, it has become a "second home" to many runners and walkers, who appreciate personal service from knowledgeable and experienced staff. Part of that feeling of home is also found when customers have the opportunity to meet other runners at any Running Room across North America. John explains: "We've had customers, particularly today, where there are so many displaced people, where they've transferred or they're fresh out of university and they don't know a soul other than the people they work with, and they can drop into the Running Room and feel instantly at home because the Wednesday runs are the same, the Sunday runs are the same." The feeling of comfort and reliability has contributed to the company's uniqueness and branding.

Consider This

▶ What are you best at? What is your Unique Selling Proposition? What could you be spending more time doing that involves your strengths? What could you spend less time doing?

▶ Entrepreneurs Peri Shawn and Patti Fasan both committed to being "the big fish in a small pond"—their target markets are highly specific (VP of sales and their teams, and executives of ceramic tile companies, prospectively). Peri says, "The more I specialize, the more business I get." In her first month coaching full-time, Peri earned more money in one month than she did all year teaching. Patti also has seen her income rise dramatically since her days as Director of a tile company.

Define Dollars and Differences

Recognition of your uniqueness may also affect the price-point of products and services you offer. In the jewelry business, for instance, millions of people produce beaded necklaces and bracelets for ten or twenty dollars. A good percentage of those people are creative and talented, yet, are unable to make a good living because they haven't recognized their uniqueness (or lack the first entrepreneurial pillar: Belief). Susan Rind remembers the point at which she made the shift to high-end jewelry. "Do I stay lower end and go by masses and just be like everyone else, making the twenty dollar jewelry which everybody can, or do I step out on a limb and say, 'I know that I'm different. I've got to trust myself that I'm different.' "

Obviously, there has to be a demand for your unique product or service in order to be priced higher, (which is where research, intuition, and trial and error come into play) but it is unfortunate how many entrepreneurs adopt middle of the road pricing for the simple reason that it is viewed as less risky. Robert Kiyosaki, of *Rich Dad* fame, advises entrepreneurs, "Always remember that the middle price may be the most comfortable but it is also the most crowded. It's hard to be outstanding when you're average."

Entrepreneurs would rather be outstanding for a select group of people, than average to many. Much recent research points to greater financial success for entrepreneurs who choose to narrow their niche and target market. Colin Bosa, president of

BOSA Properties, says his family began their billion-dollar-business framing buildings. But when they made the decision to narrow their niche and become known as the best residential high-rise developers in Vancouver's Yaletown, the company's profits and reputation skyrocketed.

Mary Cantando, author of *The Woman's Advantage*, says she experienced several benefits from narrowing her niche market. Cantando helps women entrepreneurs with medium to large businesses attract Fortune 500 accounts. Since identifying this target market she has been recognized as an expert in her field, spends less time and money on marketing and sales, and has increased her referral rate, among other benefits.

Know Your Uniqueness in Weakness

An interesting perspective on weakness came from the youngest of the entrepreneurs interviewed. At 25, Brian Takeda's humbleness about his strengths and openness about his weaknesses came as a surprise, as I had met many young entrepreneurs proclaiming their own greatness. Here was someone who was financially successful and a brilliant thinker, yet didn't possess any illusions about his ability to "do it all". In *What Happy Companies Know*, Dan Baker suggests leading from your strengths "so that you do not become frozen by fears about your weaknesses." Good advice for entrepreneurs, yet Brian repeatedly stressed that awareness of his weaknesses gave him the wherewithal to make decisions about when to outsource and when to do things himself.

Brian had very little money to finance his dream of owning a tea bar. Mortgaging his parents' house, he spent the extra money needed to make *muzi* look, feel and act the way he had envisioned it. It paid off. The interior design of his first tea bar was rated one of the top ten best design spaces in the world by the International Interior Design Association, solely due to his decision to hire exceptional designers. Brian and Mars also had a Canadian-based design company create their packaging and design, which earned the entrepreneurs two IBM Lotus Awards for "Best Packaging and Branding". With a great interior design, packaging and branding, customers flocked to *muzi* in the heart of downtown Vancouver, and remained loyal once they tried the unique, quality products (one of Brian's strengths is the creation of the tea beverages). This led customers, who were high-profile investors, to join the company, which then influenced the largest green tea company in Japan to form a joint-venture partnership with Brian and Mars. This partnership has allowed Brian to sell matcha tea to the biggest retail chains in the world, earning a percentage of every sale.

Consider This

▶ Could you use your awareness of weaknesses to your advantage? How can you come up with the funding to hire the best rather than do or be "good enough" in different areas of your business? When faced with solving a problem, many entrepreneurs remind themselves that "there's always a way." What way have you yet to explore that will lead your company to be the best at something?

When to Turn a Weakness Into A Strength

Most of the entrepreneurs agree that it's far better to focus on your strengths rather than develop weaknesses into strengths, but there were exceptions to this. Along with many entrepreneurs, Sandra Sereda says you must be effective in sales, whether it's a natural talent or not—without sales, you don't have a business. Keep in mind that great sales people view selling as finding solutions to problems or needs. This perspective may help entrepreneurs who have distorted images of sales people being pushy and overly aggressive.

Many entrepreneurs also advised creating a vision for your company, no matter what level of business you are at. Without a plan for the future, the business will eventually flounder, and no one but you can be responsible for initially deciding on the company's Big Picture.

Lastly, as Peter Legge and the majority of other business people replied, it is imperative to get along with other people. Unless you have an Internet business, which requires nothing more than staying home in your office, most entrepreneurs must acquire this skill. Wendy McClelland says that in order to build solid relationships, you first need to become comfortable speaking with people one-on-one and in a group. By doing this, you present the best possible impression of your business. People will remember their first impression of you and will link that impression directly to your business.

If you are lacking in communication skills or any of the other areas mentioned, it would be wise to take courses, read books and speak to entrepreneurs who display the specific talents and skills that could help you. I have listed recommended reading in the bibliography at the back of this book as a place to further your quest for excellence.

Bring Out the Best in Others

Going from good to best requires that entrepreneurs, as leaders of their organization, also discover the uniqueness of their employees. Brian Scudamore says he is slow to hire because he wants to determine the passions and talents of people to make sure their uniqueness is a good fit for the company. Ozzie Jurock suggests entrepreneurs commit to their staff by finding out what their passions are and what drives them as individuals. Colin Bosa, in a Vancouver Board of Trade Panel Presentation, said he asked his employees to list one hundred life and business goals, with the purpose of helping them get there. This tells employees you value them as individuals and often helps to retain them, as they are encouraged to use their talents and employ their passions. Similarly, Terry Smith says his main strength is helping others see their area of greatest potential, whether they be his managers at Brewmasters, his own children, or friends.

One way to develop this supportive skill is to take a leadership role in an association or charitable organization. Volunteer organizations need leaders who are clear about their own potential and can identify potential in others. Azim Jamal says, "Finding your key core competence and using that to your advantage, and finding other people on your team to use their core competence, really is a magical thing." A few years ago, as a volunteer chairperson of a social worker board, Azim discovered that the eight board members were burned out by answering excessive telephone calls for help by people who found themselves in desperate situations. After taking the group of eight on a retreat, Azim had each member, with the help of the group, identify a role they would be best at, based on their strengths and passions. Some chose to concentrate on youth or parents, while others honed in on issues like marital challenges. Only one person was in charge of emergency calls; allowing the others to focus their energies on other, equally needed roles, that fulfilled their interests and tapped into their "bestness." Board members became leaders and soon had over 100 volunteers working with them.

Wisdom in Action

The good-to-great companies understand that doing what you are good at will only make you good; focusing solely on what you can potentially do better than any other organization is the only path to greatness.

Jim Collins, Good to Great

It is much easier to ride a horse in the direction it's going.

Abraham Lincoln

Write down three points of action you will take after reviewing this chapter. Then reflect on the quotes above and how these words translate to action in your life.

Chapter Seven

The Gift Inside the Rock: Seeing the Future

Telus, a telecommunications company, uses "The future is friendly" in their marketing campaigns. It is designed to reassure those who are fearful of what the future may bring. With this fear often comes a hesitancy to envision a better life, and so the majority are satisfied to let others create a vision for them. This is where entrepreneurial leaders often shine, as they are able to create a vision that people believe in and are motivated by.

Brian Scudamore understands the power of vision. He vividly recalls the date (September 17, 1998) he created the vision for his company, saying to himself, "If I imagined all possibilities, where could this go?" Brian developed a five-year Painted Picture, which involved creating a North American brand where the company franchises would be in the top 30 metros on the continent. He reached that vision and went on to set another five-year goal in 2001 to do $100 million system-wide sales by 2006, saying, "We're on track to exceed that number ahead of schedule. Everyone is so aligned in our company with what we're creating and where we're going, what it's all about."

Brian and other entrepreneurs interviewed plan for the present and future by:

▶ Clarifying and Simplifying Vision

▶ Creating a Life Vision

▶ Setting Goals

▶ Developing Measuring Systems

Clarifying and Simplifying Vision

Brian advises entrepreneurs to create a vision that provides clear direction to team members about what needs to be accomplished. It may take years before you develop a long-term vision of what you want your business to be like, just as it did for Brian. In talking to Executive Coach, Mary Ellen Sanajko, the most crucial thing about vision is that you simply begin with something, even if that something is a small detail in the picture that you will eventually develop. She gives the example of tackling a garden overgrown with weeds and in need of new plants. It takes time to build the vision of what that garden will look like in five years, yet it is crucial to have at least one clear idea in mind in order to begin.

Several of the entrepreneurs differ from Brian Scudamore in that they avoid formulating a five and ten year vision, believing that the one year or even six month time frame is more effective in focusing and dealing with constant change. Regardless of the length of the vision, many advised that new entrepreneurs not get caught up in the "how" of the vision, as the "how", one year from now, will likely be much different than the "how" initially envisioned.

Vision can be simple, according to many of the entrepreneurs. John Stanton talks about starting the Running Room with a simple company vision to be the best running store in Edmonton, which, over the course of a decade, changed to encompass all of North America. Like other entrepreneurs, John says that vision is a "moving target", because so much can change in a short time. He says the important thing is to have a focused vision when you begin so you and your employees can progress with clarity and confidence.

Despite differences in the length of vision documents, most of the entrepreneurs demonstrated the pillar of Belief and the capacity to think abundantly when creating their visions. Elana Rosenfeld envisioned Kicking Horse Coffee being sold worldwide. Brian Scudamore created a goal of one billion in system-wide sales by the end of 2012 and to be in ten countries as a globally-admired brand. Wendee Lynn Cristante wants Canadian Clyde Ride to be on the ranking system for the world's most recognized brands (like Coke, Budweiser Hitch and RCMP). The ability to dream big, of course, doesn't assure anyone of success, yet this no-limit thinking is a hallmark of business owners who continue to experience exponential growth.

When vision or goals had been achieved, entrepreneurs continually raised the bar. They noted that this is essential to self and business growth. Once Dyrand Systems reached a million in sales, Trent Dyrsmid's next vision was to develop the company into a multi-million dollar company. Similarly, former Golden Valley Foods owner, Ken Funk, says you have to keep your company growing with new goals and expanding vision, giving his example of aiming for one million in sales, then five, ten, fifty, then one hundred million.

Consider This

▶ What does your vision for your business look like? Is it large enough to encompass your deepest desires for your company?

Creating a Life Vision

Although most of the entrepreneurs focused discussions of vision on their business, several were quick to point out the importance of having a vision that encompasses your whole life. Developing a vision that takes into account your relationships, spirituality, health, and recreation, leads to a greater commitment to personal balance. Every day, Brian Takeda of *muzi* sets aside time to talk with his wife—a small action that makes a big difference in his personal balance. He says his relationship with his wife has led him to be more effective in his professional life. Fondly remembering a time when his company was just a vision, Brian says, "Way back when I had this idea for *muzi*, we (he and his wife) were in university and in some hotel room and I was telling her about it. If I didn't have that relationship I don't know if I'd have the motivation and energy to come to work every day the way I do."

Another benefit to developing a holistic vision for your life is that you can plan and create experiences that balance the type of person you are or the type of activities you're engaged in on a daily basis. Financial consultant, Alphonse Seward, says he tends to be analytical and linear. To balance that, he does creative things such as making unique cards for clients celebrating special occasions. Mike Robinson of Ultra Span Structures says his business solving structural problems is solitary; his volunteer work, as District Governor of Toastmasters, is social, with many meetings, phone calls and conferences. Because the contrast between the two activities is so sharp, Mike says he has no difficulty managing the two throughout the workday, and is able to switch gears with little effort.

▶ My Story

While writing this book, I took on the planning and execution of a major fundraiser for my son's preschool. Gathering silent auction items and selling tickets forced me to get out of my house and meet many people—something I needed to balance the daily isolation of writing. Until I spoke with Mike Robinson and some of the other entrepreneurs, I had never really thought about purposely doing activities that are opposite of what you spend most of your day doing. This new awareness has created personal harmony and enthusiasm for visiting a blank page every morning.

Consider This

▶ What is your vision of a balanced life? List each aspect, and determine what you need to do to move toward your vision.

▶ What contrasting activities or experiences can provide you with work/life balance? How much time are you willing to commit to these in order to reach your vision of a balanced life?

Observations on Mission Statements

Nowhere were the entrepreneurs more divided in opinion than on the topic of mission statements. While some clearly connected their focus and commitment to their mission, others simply didn't view this practice as essential to their personal or professional success.

Mission statements have long been used in companies to help define what the ultimate purpose of the organization is. Unfortunately, many employees don't embrace it, and often, as Ozzie Jurock says, "they couldn't even tell you what its basic premise is."

One of the biggest Canadian-owned franchises, 1-800-GOT-JUNK?, doesn't use mission statements. Brian Scudamore explains, "I don't believe in writing something out and saying, 'Here's our mission.' I believe if you've got the right people based on the company's cultural fit, or a values-based fit, and a vision to know what you're trying to accomplish, that's really what you need." With system-wide sales surpassing a set goal of 70 million in 2005, Scudamore's company clearly isn't impeded by a lack of mission statements.

Some entrepreneurs stressed that in the first few years of business, so much changes, that mission statements made six months ago may not be relevant today. Willingness to accept this and be adaptable was a strength that all the entrepreneurs exhibited. Wendee Lynn Cristante illustrated this adaptability and openness to opportunity when her Canadian Clyde Ride team participated in the annual Rose Bowl parade in 2005. Prior to this event, Wendee's mission was to change people's views of Clydesdales being slow and heavy-footed workhorses by turning them into show horses that perform complex, quick-footed maneuvers. Her mission changed after witnessing the warmth and enthusiasm Americans displayed when her team, carrying the Canadian flag and adorned in red and white, circled the stadium. Familiar with luke-warm response to the nation's flag at local venues, Wendee says, "Canadians need to be more appreciative of who we are and what we're about ... I want to bring more pride to our country, and if I can display that through my horses and the flag and my team, that's my goal."

Those who believe in the value of mission statements were quick to add that the document need not be long and complex. A brief one-sentence statement helped these entrepreneurs keep the "why" of the business in mind. Laura Prosko, of Prosko Group Productions Inc., has as her mission, "To bring people together for events." Powerful in its conciseness! John Stanton's initial vision has evolved into the Running Room's mission statement: "To be the best running and walking store in North America." John points out that "best" is not just from a retail standpoint, but best means having the best people doing the best things in the community, like organizing and hosting runs for various health-related charities. He notes, "It's a very simplistic statement, yet it embraces the whole culture of the company."

Like John, others stressed that mission statements are only valuable if designed by the entire team of employees. With a whole-team approach, mission statements survive the transition into the company's values and culture. Sandra Sereda understands this transition well. She explains that there's no ownership by the workers if they have no say as to what goes into the document. She gives the example of a statement within her mission that involves promoting from within, a policy that few fast food companies live by, but one that has increased employee retention in her stores. Even those who take a hiatus often return to the company and are welcomed with open arms.

▶ **My Story**

In the beginning stages of my journey as an info-preneur, I met a business consultant who asked what my mission statement was. When I told him I didn't have one, he shook his head in disappointment, saying, "You will never have a sense of direction and achieve personal or professional success without one." Stunned, I went home and thought about how "experts" in business or self-development cause anxiety as people think they must do things precisely in the prescribed fashion. Elana Rosenfeld agrees, saying she doesn't care for the emphasis placed on mission statements. Like many other entrepreneurs, she explained that things change so quickly in her business that she finds values and beliefs to be a far greater guide to focus and decision-making than mission statements.

Consider This

▶ Take some time to reflect on the importance of a mission statement for your company. If you have one already, do you revisit it occasionally and reflect upon its value to you and the people in your company?

Setting Goals

Goal setting is one entrepreneurial practice consistent with the advice of self-development experts. Everyone talked about the power of goal setting: announcing goals to others, posting goals in high traffic areas, and carrying goals in wallets and purses. The longest-held goal was Farah Perelmuter's, who, as a child, had an entrepreneurial dream that was realized at the exact time of my interview with her. "My dream was to have an office in Toronto where the elevator opens right into the office. There's a glass desk, and I can see the CN Tower from my window. So, as of Friday, we get the office of our dreams and it has those three elements in it." Reaching long-held goals is magical, but even the achievement of short-term goals can feel wonderful. In his early twenties, Trent Dyrsmid of Dyrand Systems set a year-long income goal of 100,000 dollars, despite being unemployed and uncertain as to what business he would create. This goal was met and slightly surpassed: 102,000 dollars—a number Trent says may be coincidence—or proof of the forces at work which help us achieve what we make known to ourselves and the world.

Several entrepreneurs suggested visualizing goals and a broader business vision. Farah Perelmuter, in holding on to her childhood dream, continually imagined what her office would look like, with all the textures, sights and sounds. Her experience resonates with Brian Scudamore, who every five years creates what he calls the "Painted Picture"—a vision of what his company will look like, feel like and act like. Using multiple senses was not a common experience amongst all people interviewed, but for those who do visualize fully, company and personal goals are vivid and take on a life of their own. Visualized dreams also remind people of their purpose and passion when challenges arise. Distractions tend to be minimalized, while focus is heightened.

Developing Measuring Systems

What provides even greater focus in goal setting is creating a system to measure your goals. Brian Scudamore believes, "What gets measured or monitored gets changed." One of his managers cites an example of this, where the call center's "closing percentage" (number of calls becoming actual customers) went up by as much as ten percent when a daily focus was placed on monitoring it. Ten percent in a year for a company with hundreds of franchises translates to millions of dollars. Employees not only have access to this information, but have ownership in contributing to the measuring and analysis of it. Because of this, any adjustments towards achieving goals are truly a team effort, and the company, despite its tremendous size, can act quickly.

Imagine monitoring goals in all areas of our lives—how much more effective we could be! **Creating systems to monitor personal and professional goals keeps us accountable to the values we believe in, the kind of person we want to become, and the impact we wish to have in business and society.** When people participate in my seminars, they find it easy to measure financial goals, but far more difficult to measure goals in areas of life that don't involve numbers. Once they are able to measure these goals, they feel empowered to monitor their growth and make changes.

Living in the moment is a goal that many people aspire to, yet most people don't reach, in part, because they lack systems to monitor progress. I discovered one creative way that works for me: every time I catch myself not being fully present when I need to be, I pinch the back of my elbow, and record the number of times I do this in one day. While a little uncomfortable, it isn't self-punishment. It is, as Sylvia Taylor says, an "attention getter" for your brain. She gives a similar example of snapping a rubber band on your wrist to note negative thoughts or anxiety and phobias. Such methods help monitor, over days and weeks, progress towards a goal. A little bit of creativity and even playfulness may help you come up with monitoring tools to reach goals.

Consider This

▶ Do you have an effective way of measuring and monitoring your progress in reaching goals? Do you do this in all areas of your life? What part of your life can you commit to monitoring or measuring today? What would this mean to your business and life-balance?

Wisdom in Action

Your present circumstances don't determine where you can go, they merely determine where you start.

Nido Qubein

Because all things are created twice, if you don't take charge of the first creation, someone or something else will.

Stephen Covey

Write down three points of action you will take after reviewing this chapter. Then reflect on the quotes above and how these words translate to action in your life.

Chapter Eight

Polishing State of Mind

A dominant theme emerging from interviews was the impact of thought, attitude, and state of mind on business success. Some entrepreneurs experienced the power of their thoughts as positive turning points in their business and life. Some had to recuperate from a downward spiral of negativity and depression in order to begin a new business. Either way, most mentioned some or all of the following tools as significant in the sculpting of their business and entrepreneurial selves:

▶ Practicing Optimism

▶ Accepting Abundance

▶ Celebrating and Giving Thanks

▶ Seeing Opportunity

▶ Capitalizing on Problems

▶ Taking Responsibility

▶ Resisting Instant Gratification

Practicing Optimism

You've likely known, or heard of, outrageously successful people who don't appear to have an ounce of optimism in them—not pleasant to be around, but proof that optimism isn't always necessary in meeting business goals. Nevertheless, it is an ingredient that many entrepreneurs deem necessary to their personal success, particularly in times of challenge or when starting a new business.

Some entrepreneurs confessed that despite being viewed as optimistic, they had times when they too struggled to maintain a bright outlook. This comes as a shock to people who believe others are just blessed with a great attitude. Tami Reilly says she constantly feeds her positive thinking by reading motivational books and listening to tapes that help maintain perspective and energy. Marketing expert, Wendy McClelland, who once struggled with depression, avoids newspapers and will switch channels when news is too negative. In *Developing the Leader Within You*, John Maxwell talks about seeing some motivational quotes in his dad's briefcase. Since his dad always had a great attitude, John asked, "Are you still reading that stuff?" and his dad replied, "Son, I have to keep working on my thought-life. I am responsible to have a great attitude and to maintain it. My attitude does not run on automatic." Similarly, author Og Mandino asserts his belief in feeding the Self with positive dreams and images in *The Greatest Miracle in the World*. Og expresses his ideas through a fictional character, who says, "Reading any twenty-minute-passage once will do little good, but reading that same message each night, before you go to sleep, opens many hidden passages in your mind." Maintaining motivation, energy and optimism is achievable, and with daily focus, can strengthen self-belief and commitment to goals and vision.

Optimism is also critical in dealing with customers. Brenda Alberts, Birthplace of B.C. Gallery owner, sells original paintings and says that one key to her success has been remaining positive. She notes that when there is anxiety or worry, customers can sense this, and won't buy. She gives the example of breaking her leg, and watching sales plummet as customers sensed not only her anxiety, but her physical pain as well. These people simply stopped coming to the gallery for a period of time, and she ended up losing substantial sales during the time her leg was in a cast.

Several other entrepreneurs also talked about avoiding any talk of mental or physical pain with employees. Ozzie Jurock advises entrepreneurs not to reveal worries to employees. "Quite often in small business we tell our people all our worries, but they have their own worries. Your job is to be strong. While they may be sympathetic talking to you about it, in the end, they will be pushed away from you. They want to see that you have vision. Good people want to be attracted to a strong person."

Farah and Martin Perelmuter, of Speakers' Spotlight, needed to be the visionaries. Together, they needed to be that strong person on September 11, 2001. Just one day before tragedy struck, Farah and Martin had received a contract to move into a larger office seven times the rent of their former location. They accepted the financial risk that day, but while watching the news in horror, asked themselves, "Are we going to slip into this risk? Who knows what's going to happen to the conferences our clients are putting on?" Despite their fears, they went on to sign the agreement because they ultimately believed in the future, and more importantly, wanted their employees and clients to believe in it too. The following months were frighteningly slow, Farah admits, but eventually the cancelled conferences were rescheduled and business returned to normal.

Accepting Abundance

Farah and Martin's story is an example of not only believing in yourself and your team, but in the abundance of the world—that there will be enough business to be financially successful. With earning income, there is an attitude of unlimited potential, rather than anxiety of whether there is enough to go around. This belief applies to their relationships as well. When Sweat Co. owner, Maureen Wilson, presents at fitness conferences, people are amazed at the depth and detail of the information she shares, thanking her for wisdom collected over two decades. They often reveal they aren't used to presenters willing to share success tips and detailed handouts. Maureen's attitude also extends to competitors. She helped a former employee get a workout studio up and running and continues to mentor another entrepreneur in the same industry.

▶ My Story

When I worked as a manager for a top direct-sales company, I was shocked by the number of people who didn't believe in the abundance of the world. For every individual setting sales or recruiting records, there were people making hundreds of excuses as to why that person performed so well. Yet for every excuse, there were several thousand sales people happily proving them wrong. The instant I heard these excuses, I knew such naysayers would likely be doing something else within a year's time; something that didn't require abundant thinking, courage, vision, or, as Ozzie Jurock would say, "a commitment to a self-actualized life."

Susan Rind is also no stranger to a giving attitude. When Susan gave out 35 of her exclusive dragonfly pins in a tribute to her mentor, Ella Little, people were stunned by her generosity. (Perhaps this is one of the reasons Oprah's popularity continues to soar.) Susan called her gift-giving "a random act of kindness", asking women to think of passing on the kindness whenever they wore their pins.

In the creative realm, Susan's acceptance and trust in an abundant world impacts the production side of her business. Because she needs to create different collections of jewelry every season, she goes through the same fears many entrepreneurs do—she wonders if she can come up with enough ideas to complete her goal. Every season, however, her fears are unfounded, as she continues to produce one-of-a-kind jewelry. Writer Annie Dillard brilliantly sums up the experience of creative abundance:

> "One of the few things I know about writing is this: spend it all, shoot it, play it, lose it, all, right away, every time. Do not hoard what seems good for a latter place in the book, or for another book; give it, give it all, give it now. The impulse to save something good for a better place later is the signal to spend it now. Something more will arise for later, something better."

Celebrating and Giving Thanks

With the belief in an abundant world also comes a sense of gratitude and celebration for what the entrepreneurs do have. This may be obvious to some, but Farah Perelmuter of Speakers' Spotlight notes that it is easy to neglect present-moment gratitude. At the time of my interview with Farah, she and husband Martin had just reached a major business goal, and for the first time, she didn't have another goal. Her emphasis was on enjoying and being grateful for the goal that they did reach, knowing that new goals would be set and achieved later.

Farah's comment sparked a curiosity about the significance of celebration. If we practice gratitude on a daily basis, it also needs to extend into gratitude for our own achievements. Executive Coach, Mary Ellen Sanajko, says that celebration is often undervalued and overlooked in our life journey. However, it is an important part of renewing motivation, self-belief and commitment to action.

Extending celebration and gratitude into company culture directly impacts employee health, happiness, and company growth, as shown in *How Full is Your Bucket? Positive Strategies for Work and Life.* Authors Tom Rath and Donald Clifton surveyed more than four million employees worldwide, and found that "individuals who receive recognition and praise increase individual productivity, increase engagement among their colleagues, are more likely to stay with their organization, receive higher loyalty and satisfaction scores from customers, have better safety records and have fewer accidents on the job."

Consider This

▶ In what ways do you demonstrate an attitude of abundance? In what ways do you celebrate your personal and company advancements, big or small? If you committed to one small change today, what would it be and how would it impact different areas of your life?

▶ Experiment with an Appreciation Journal, listing ten things you are grateful for every day for thirty days. Reflect on the impact this has on your life.

Seeing Opportunity

Part of the abundant thinker's traits is the ability to recognize and act on business opportunities. Sometimes the opportunities involve the passions or interests of entrepreneurs, but not always. As is sometimes the case with entrepreneurs, opportunity arose from personal needs that translated into a niche market.

As a young father, John Stanton was asked to participate in a run with his children. An out-of-shape and overweight smoker, he could barely jog to the end of his street. To manage the three-kilometer run with his children, he decided to change his sedentary lifestyle and become a model of health for his family. When he discovered that he couldn't find anyone who was knowledgeable enough to help him find a good pair of runners, he researched everything there was to know about running, became a self-taught expert, and eventually competed in marathons and Iron Man events. While becoming passionate about running, John recognized the opportunity for a business that would fill a niche—a place where runners could seek expert advice, not only on getting the right pair of shoes, but also on training for marathons and learning about running programs, nutrition and goal setting.

Similarly, Tami Reilly's business was born from a need to effectively organize her leasing business. When she recognized that many people were in equally desperate circumstances and wanted assistance, she actively built a loyal customer base as an office organizer. Wendee Lynn Cristante, of Canadian Clyde Ride, says her business arose from a passion for Clydesdales. Her love of the gentle giants led her to show the skeptical world that they could in fact be show horses. Whether opportunities arise from an existing passion or a perceived need, the entrepreneurs who act on these opportunities are rewarded.

This reward is often perceived as pure luck, yet many of the entrepreneurs know 'luck' is a combination of several factors. Susan Rind says good fortune is more likely to come your way when you have clear intentions for your business. This is similar to ideas on intuition and serendipity, where entrepreneurs who have clear vision or goals, frequently experience intuitive guidance. In *The Spontaneous Fulfillment of Desire*, Deepak Chopra says that the "good luck formula" is "opportunity plus preparedness", and that it is possible, "to create such a state of mind that you will begin to see that there are opportune moments in life, and when you notice and take hold of them, they change everything."

Ozzie Jurock told me that he lives a charmed life, full of good fortune, but when I examined the experiences and words of this real estate expert and how open he is to taking on challenges and exploring opportunities, I wasn't surprised at his extensive "good luck". From selling all his property and moving to Mexico just before interest rates went sky-high in the early 80's to becoming the president of Royal LePage Asia in Taiwan in the 90's, Ozzie's preparedness in the world of real estate beckoned "good luck" when opportunities presented themselves. Now he is touted as one of the smartest "money people" around by self-development experts like Mark Victor Hansen, of *Chicken Soup for the Soul* fame.

In *The Luck Factor*, Dr. Richard Wiseman summarizes the results of hundreds of studies he conducted of lucky and unlucky people in the context of chance opportunities, concluding that there are key attributes or actions that define the lucky: they build strong networks and relationships, they have a relaxed attitude (thereby noticing more opportunities), and they are open to new experiences in their lives. Not surprisingly, this description fits Ozzie and most of the entrepreneurs I interviewed. Like Ozzie, they used the word "lucky" to describe themselves and the opportunities they capitalized on.

Seasoned entrepreneurs also believe that opportunity and observation go hand in hand. Marketing expert, Wendy McClelland, says she doesn't have a business degree nor any special training in marketing. What she does have is the power of observation. She notes,

> "I know what's going on in popular culture, I read a lot, I watch different types of TV shows, from MSN and CNN to Much Music. I am immersed in the culture of society and am aware of the trends and psychology of marketing. I am an observer of human nature and am able to translate that into something that's going to create business."

When Wendy first discovered the Internet, for instance, she was so fascinated by the business opportunities available that she literally did not sleep for two nights. A few months later, Wendy's business resource website was listed by *The New York Times* as one of the best on the Internet.

Capitalizing on Problems

While I have presented many stories of good fortune, there are times when all entrepreneurs experience unwelcome change. Their attitude and corresponding actions, however, have clearly made a difference in their business success. In *What Happy Companies Know*, Dan Baker says most companies display problem-centered thinking rather than opportunity-centered thinking, leading to excessive fire fighting and a consequent lack of creative, fresh ideas. The entrepreneurs interviewed were clearly opportunity-centered thinkers, even when faced with tremendous obstacles.

When Trent Dyrsmid was deeply in debt trying to get Dyrand Systems off the ground, he would gaze out his office window and see a steady stream of women going to a spa. Rather than bemoan the possibility that he might not pull out of debt, Trent recognized the opportunity in providing women with products they desire. A few months later, his thoughts were turned into a lucrative on-line jewelry business.

Threatening circumstances also surrounded Golden Valley Foods several times, shares former owner and CEO, Ken Funk. One challenge began in the Spring of 2004, when the Avian Flu hit the Vancouver Lower Mainland. A large area of farms was chosen for depopulation, and Ken's supply of eggs dropped by seventy-five percent. Ken and his staff put together a plan that involved transporting eggs across the Canada/US border, but they needed to get the support of competitors, government and other egg producers across the country. No easy task. Yet with his belief that there's always a way, Ken and his team did sell the plan to the other groups involved and were able to save the jobs of every employee and supply every customer.

Consider This

▶ The Chinese ideogram for crisis also means opportunity. How do you want to be in the good times? In the hard times? What quality do you want to call forth?

Taking Responsibility

In order to deal with the inevitable struggles and stages businesses go through, an attitude of self-responsibility is necessary. Unfortunately, many people indulge in the "complain and blame" game, which robs them of a self-actualized life. In Jack Canfield's *The Success Principles*, he says, "Complaining means you have a reference point for something better that you would prefer but that you are unwilling to take the risk of creating. Either accept that you are making the choice to stay where you are, take responsibility for your choice, and stop complaining ... or ... take the risk of creating your life exactly the way you want it." Rather than Ken Funk blaming government or industry regulators for the problems Golden Valley Foods faced, he asked himself what he and his team could do that would be the best-case scenario for all involved, and then followed through on that plan.

Avoiding problem-centred thinking in favour of personal responsibility is a shared trait of many entrepreneurs in the way they view both challenges and opportunities. Trent Dyrsmid says:

"I see things differently than most people. People look at something on the street and their intuitive response will be why it won't work, and I was the same way, where I'll say now, 'What would I need to do to make it work?' And as subtle as that is to say, the reality of that one simple change of thinking is huge. You can't even really state how big that is ... That's the difference between being an employee and being a billionaire."

Trent clearly understands that the questions successful entrepreneurs ask lead to a self-actualized life, where there is little room for excuses, blame and negativity.

For many entrepreneurs interviewed, part of taking personal responsibility involves being willing to constantly learn and grow, in business and other areas of life. Darren McDowell uses a powerful metaphor to explain the importance of growth. "I see all these different wheels; here's sales, here's the accounting department, here's idea development, the employee division, but up here is the oil can oiling it. The Oil Can is educating yourself, constantly making sure the wheels are all working together, keeping things moving."

This self-education can involve simply taking the time to think deeply. For Peri Shawn, clear thinking is one of her greatest skills, whether she is developing products, reflecting on progress toward goals, or solving problems. Founder of the *Canadian Immigrant Magazine*, Nick Noorani, says he takes 90 minutes every morning to think about where his company is headed and the steps he must take to get there. Albert Einstein once explained his discovery of the Theory of Relativity by saying, "It's not that I'm so smart, it's just that I stay with problems longer." In today's fast-paced world, taking the time to think and reflect is crucial to company growth.

Some of the entrepreneurs considered books to be an essential part of the Oil Can.

Several owners of successful businesses talked about Michael Gerber's *The E-Myth* as being the single most influential book in structuring their businesses. Gerber explains how to create effective businesses based on a franchise model. When Tami Reilly, of GO Get Organized, began her business as an office organizer, she read and re-read *The E-Myth*:

> "I thought, 'If I'm going to start a business, I'm going to do it in a way that has the highest propensity for success. And I thought that studying the *E-Myth* was a good idea, because if I enjoyed getting businesses organized and that's all I did, then I would be what Gerber calls a 'technician'. What I really wanted was to be an entrepreneur with a business concept that was duplicatable."

Tami went on to perfect the systems she created in order to license others as office organizers in her company. She is now most proud of her customer retention and selling more to fewer people, as a by-product of carefully devised systems.

According to Brian Scudamore, the success of 1-800-GOT-JUNK? is also largely due to having picked up Gerber's classic. Brian had been running his business for several years when the logic of *The E-Myth* spoke to his deepest desires:

> "The reason it had such a big impact on me is, I said, 'I want to scale my business. I want to look at putting systems in place.' Michael's belief is that people don't fail, systems do. If you've got the right system in place, you can build a scaleable organization. Two years into it, by 1997, my business started to look, feel, and act so much like a franchise that I said, 'You know what, maybe

that's something I should look at.' And I did and no looking back."

The E-Myth has also been useful for business owners who have experienced quick growth with no systems to adapt to that growth. Wendy McClelland says she learned this lesson from the late Internet marketing genius, Corey Rudl. He explained to her that carefully devised systems help keep wildly successful novices on the right track, giving the example of his own Internet business which grew too big, too fast, with no systems in place to account for growth. After this experience, Corey took two weeks away from work to set up intricate systems for every level of his business. He advised Wendy to do the same, as most entrepreneurs he knew didn't fail because they were unsuccessful—they failed because they were too successful.

The most frequently discussed Oil Can tool was talking to business people experiencing success in areas the entrepreneurs struggled with. Rick Jongkind, a senior executive for a direct sales company, says that he practices the wisdom of "When you're down, look up and when you're up, look down," noting that, "When people are down, they cocoon. They just put a shell around themselves. That's the wrong time to do it. You've got to look for somebody that's succeeding or that's up in life, where you aspire to be. You've got to reach out, as uncomfortable as that may be."

Trent Dyrsmid is not afraid to reach out. Whether struggling to keep a business going or starting a new one, Trent's motto is "Wisdom is just a phone call away." When he wanted to begin his business selling products on-line, he looked at the websites of people who were successful and gave them a call. They were more than happy to share their wisdom.

Although most business people respond positively to advice-seekers, not everyone is comfortable asking questions, as Laura Prosko found out on returning to Canada, after spending several years studying and working in the United States. While in the US, she found that people encouraged her to live her dream and not be afraid to seek information necessary to help actualize that dream. On returning to Canada, however, she found many people hesitant to admit ignorance, particularly where money was concerned. "I found that people are scared to talk about money," she says, giving the example of new and experienced entrepreneurs in a roundtable discussion where the neophytes were asking very few questions. When Laura asked about finances in year-one of business, different conversations about money suddenly began, illustrating the need to ask questions, especially uncomfortable ones, in order to learn and grow.

As a teenager supporting herself and living on her own, one of Maureen Wilson's survival mechanisms was to ask questions. Now, as owner of Sweat Co., Maureen believes in asking questions about all aspects of her business. From meeting with city planners, to discussing liability with insurance brokers, to reviewing procedures with her accountant, Maureen asks questions necessary to keep her business healthy. Often, these professionals are shocked by the number and types of questions she asks, saying that most people don't bother to gain a thorough understanding, and leave responsibility to others.

This abdication of responsibility can be disastrous, as Eric Huang observes in many Chinese restaurants. He says that failure to understand every aspect of your business puts others in control, which leads to suppliers and employees making many of the decisions that you should be. He gives the example of restaurants where owners have no idea how to prepare the food, so cooks and suppliers become controlling, knowing that owners are in a vulnerable position.

Resisting Instant Gratification

Part of taking responsibility as a business owner is committing to the growth of your business over time. That means accepting the peaks and the valleys, accepting the cyclical nature of business, and knowing that not everything we do has immediate results.

Eight years ago, as an award-winning manager with Discovery Toys, I flew first class to Orlando for a sales incentive vacation. During this flight, I sat next to an elderly man with a crisp white shirt and pinstriped business suit. His business was manufacturing doors—100,000 a day. When I asked him what the secret to his success was, he simply replied, "I didn't quit." He went on to explain that many of his friends, and even one of his entrepreneurial children, gave up too easily. In a world of instant gratification, our culture has become so fixated on the "getting it now" expectation that major challenges are rarely worked through. The great majority of 50–75 year old entrepreneurs I interviewed said the idea of quitting, rarely, if ever, entered their psyche. It simply wasn't an option.

Entrepreneur Sandra Sereda developed a snack food called Tessa's Pita Chips. Her friends loved the chips and eagerly advised her to sell them, saying it would be an easy way to make money. She laughs, remembering all the tribulations involved in putting the product on the shelves of major grocery stores. "It's one step forward, four steps back—but there's always a way," she adds. "There's always a way," peppered the conversations I had with entrepreneurs, emphasizing the wisdom of continually working through obstacles.

In 1974, Ella Little moved from small-town Saskatchewan to Vancouver's Lower Mainland. Within weeks of moving, the forty-two-year-old single mother of four negotiated a straight trade of a modest travel trailer for a storefront called "Faith's Fashions". The name says it all, she laughs, remembering the dismal inventory. Yet, she pointed out, "I didn't consider not making it work. It's something I had to do." With no option other than to succeed, Ella never allowed herself to travel the road of doubt and defeat. Even today, at 73, she personally attends to her customers five days a week.

Peter Legge shares Ella's philosophy of never giving up. One of the top speakers in North America, the sixty-four-year-old Legge says he is often asked by prospective speakers what it takes to become a great speaker. His advice is to speak whenever and wherever you can. Speak for free. He makes the analogy of an Olympic athlete: "Does an Olympic athlete run just once every four years? If you want to be a gold-medal speaker, then you do what it takes."

Doing what it takes, no matter how difficult, certainly separates the business 'athlete' from the business 'couch-potato', but also does something even more important: it lessens the impact of fear and failure. Those who do what it takes are willing to move through fear and failure for a chance at success. Making the decision to do what it takes is making a long-term commitment to growing your business.

Some Sculpting Advice

As a beginning entrepreneur, the number of things you need to learn can be overwhelming, but three points of advice were given: the first is stated above—to ask questions and know that many entrepreneurs will be generous in assisting you. The second is to take action after asking these questions, regardless of whether you adopt or adapt the advice given. Begin today, because some mistakes, as Brian Takeda says, are lesson fees—we need to make them in order to continue to grow and become the best we can be. Too many people become paralyzed by the enormity of the learning curve, and never begin. Publisher Arielle Ford's newsletter states that the number one reason books never get written is because people don't know where to start. There are so many elements in putting a book together that people never begin.

A final point of advice, from Rick Jongkind, is that small daily improvements are more effective than making a big leap every few months. Rick often shares his belief that: "Those things that are extraordinary today, will become ordinary tomorrow." For example, people marvel at Jerry Seinfeld's seemingly effortless ability to do stand-up comedy, and yet those who work closely with him say that he is constantly trying out new material and presenting it in different ways to different audiences to get it right. We don't see the small daily improvements of those who are the very best in their field, and forget that self-growth is more about what we do every day.

This concept can be seen in educational practices in different parts of the world. North Americans tend to place far less value on daily practice in the pursuit of greatness, preferring to be in awe of talent. In many Asian countries, however, practice is highly valued—the discipline of daily acts towards a cumulative result. The great musical educator and performer, Sinichi Suzuki, always professed to have little talent, but was determined to practice regularly. His personal experience influenced millions of families who use his music programs today.

Consider This

▶ Mother Teresa understood the concept of seemingly unimportant, daily acts. A young man once approached her, eager to help India's poor. "What can I do to become a more loving person?" he asked. She replied, "Do small things with great love."

▶ Doing small things with greatness is something all entrepreneurs can achieve. What small daily things, done with greatness, will change your business and life?

Wisdom in Action

People make a mistake who think that my art has come easily to me. Nobody has devoted so much time and thought to composition as I. There is not a famous master whose music I have not studied over and over.

Wolfgang Amadeus Mozart

What do I think about when I strike out? I think about hitting home runs.

Babe Ruth

Write down three points of action you will take after reviewing this chapter. Then reflect on the quotes above and how these words translate to action in your life.

Part Three

Relationships and the Heart of the Sculptor

It's much more fun being the David than being the Goliath.

Sir Richard Branson

Chapter Nine

The *I Like You* Principle

When entrepreneurs were asked what influences their success more than anything else, the most common response was developing strong relationships. Peter Legge says, "The ability to get along with other men and women is the cornerstone of anybody's success, no matter what industry they're in." Approximately 70 percent of all employees are fired because they cannot get along with other people. Roughly the same percentage of employees leave companies because they dislike their boss. These statistics speak to the urgency of developing better relationship skills to promote healthier and happier workplaces.

Terry Smith says his ability to get along with others is his greatest strength. As a young man selling medical equipment, he was not the brightest or most talented individual in the company, yet he was continually offered executive positions in the company because he was great to work with. Terry's relationships with co-workers and clients was so strong that after a few years, he no longer needed to make cold calls, relying solely on referrals and repeat business. Terry believes this success was largely due to his genuine interest in helping clients reach their medical research goals versus selling them a piece of equipment. Scientists and researchers began to trust that he wasn't just out to make the sale, and that he was truly eager to learn from and help them in their quest for the best technology available.

Farah Perelmuter says she and husband Martin's people-skills have been a decisive factor in the huge success of Speakers' Spotlight. She advises other entrepreneurs: "You need to create excellent relationships with clients so that you build loyalty; create excellent relationships with your employees so that they want to work for you and do the best job possible; and create great relationships with your supplier, because inevitably, you're going to ask them for a favour."

But what does "building relationships" really involve? What skills can entrepreneurs develop to strengthen this relationship quotient? As I asked entrepreneurs these questions, the following character traits and communication skills emerged, which I call the *I Like You* Principle. The **character traits** include:

▶ Love of People

▶ Inner Peace

▶ Being Non-Judgemental

The **communication skills** include:

▶ Clarity and Conciseness

▶ Being a Straight Shooter

▶ Persuasiveness

▶ Asking Questions

▶ Listening

Love of People

As simple as it sounds, this principle may be the most compelling element in successful business relationships. World-class speaker, Peter Legge, illustrates his love for people when he mingles with his audience for over half an hour prior to going on stage. When I said that many other speakers don't do this, he replied, "I just do it because I think it's the right thing to do. I do it instinctively. I don't just do it for effect. I do it because I think 'I want to meet you.'"

Real estate guru Ozzie Jurock says, "It is basic things that make me successful, and that is that I really care about people. I really want to know what they do. When I go to a cafeteria, I want to know where they all come from, and what the dishwasher does and what they all do." In the mid-eighties, Ozzie was president of Royal Lepage Canada, and noted that Quebec realtors hadn't seen a company president for five years, although they had 130 branches. With the little French he spoke, Ozzie made the effort to find out more about them and work with them. Not surprisingly, they adored their new leader and this eventually led the company to offer Ozzie the job of president of Royal LePage Asia.

Dale Carnegie once said, "You can make more friends in two months by becoming interested in other people than you can in two years by trying to get other people interested in you." Peter and Ozzie's genuine love of people has directly impacted their success with many business acquaintances. This likeability leads to a host of other benefits, including more business referrals, mentoring opportunities, and an overall positive impact on the community.

When people know you are genuinely interested in them, they begin to reciprocate your positive energies. Maureen Wilson, owner of Sweat Co. and a personal trainer, sees this happen frequently with clients. They see her passion for fitness and her excitement for helping them reach their goals, and they become far more energetic and positive. She notes that in one-on-one training, clients often divulge personal challenges because they just need someone to listen to them, and don't always arrive full of energy and enthusiasm. Because she cares for them as people, she makes the effort to pass on her energy and love, and they become long-term clients.

As part of their love of people, many entrepreneurs talked about their belief in the inner power of people. Maureen Wilson believes everyone contains huge reserves of untapped potential— what she and other entrepreneurs thrive on when working with people. Rick Jongkind says, "I believe in people. I believe there's greatness in everybody. The world teaches them that they're not."

Terry Smith uses this same "greatness" philosophy in seeking out the potential in others that they don't know they have. This self-initiative has made Terry one of the most beloved entrepreneurs and city councilors in Langley, British Columbia. Zig Ziglar's famous quote, "People don't care what you know until they know how much you care," applies to Terry's life. Whether participating in community functions as city councilor, serving patrons in his Brewmasters store, or inviting locals for coffee at McBurney's, a coffee house he rents, Terry can be spotted having lively conversations with Langley residents because he genuinely cares for people.

This type of caring also results in entrepreneurs keeping in touch with the needs and concerns of both customers and staff. John Stanton of the Running Room is a tremendous role model for this concept of connection, as he spends over eighty percent of his time in the 87 stores he and his two sons, John and Jason, own and operate. This allows him to learn, firsthand, about strengths and potential problems. It also helps him maintain the caring culture of the Running Room, where employees and even customers, know the president and feel comfortable communicating with him.

One of the most recognizable presidents of a Canadian family-owned company, John has touched thousands of lives by being accessible and available to the public. He notes that some people might think he has a huge ego because his photo is prominent throughout his organization, including his books, magazine, catalogue and website. His intention is to connect with the customer. "I want everyone who shops in our store to know that if they need to get ahold of somebody, they know who to go to. If they feel frustrated over something and they feel they haven't been treated fairly, they can call me. My telephone number is there, my e-mail address is there."

Top executive coach, Graham Alexander, advises similar practices in his book, *Tales From The Top*: "Check your daily agenda for the percentage of time you spend with customers. If you cannot remember the last time you spoke with a customer, you're out of touch." John told me about fitting a customer for shoes a few days prior to our interview because staff got busy. He takes frequent opportunities to do book signings in his stores and joins marathons and running/walking events as an athlete, to stay close to the heart and soul of his customers. The extra effort John commits to has paid off— his stores have customers who come in several times a week, whether to get a dose of motivation, to research an upcoming event, or to check out the latest innovations in running.

Many entrepreneurs also spend a great deal of time with staff, not because they have to, but, because they want to. Several entrepreneurs I interviewed referred to their employees as "family", saying they are grateful not only for the immense skill of employees, but also appreciate their attitudes, values, and, at times, friendship. Ella Little, when asked why many of her employees have worked for her for well over a decade, replied, "I love them. I absolutely love them." Ella explains that her staff respects each other's idiosyncrasies and appreciate each other's differences, rather than dwelling on the "why can't you be more like me" attitudes prevalent in many businesses. The entrepreneurs who have the ability to get along with their employees generally are those who value different perspectives and ways of doing things.

Maureen Wilson and Farah Perelmuter take their staff to events such as live theater productions and Yuk Yuks to show appreciation and to connect with them on a personal level. The late George Preston enjoyed his more than 100 employees so much he talked to them daily and knew them all by name. When showing me the various areas of his car dealership, George told me of an employee who returned to work after her maternity leave because of a thoughtful gesture: he created a nursery in her office where she could have the flexibility to be a part-time worker and a full-time mom. Only entrepreneurs with a genuine love of people would take action to give employees choices like this.

Inner Peace

People are often attracted to qualities in others they have a hard time developing in themselves. Perhaps one of the most difficult qualities to achieve in today's world is inner peace. With more people working longer and harder and taking on more family obligations, it seems to be further from our grasp than ever before. When entrepreneurs have it, however, others sense it and want to be a part of it.

Rick and Jacqueline Jongkind are living examples of reaching a state of true peace. Rick says he often has people tell him that he and Jacqueline embody this elusive state. In fact, one individual wanted to know what business they are involved in, not because of his interest in direct sales, but because he saw the whole package the Jongkind family represents to him: harmony, joy, and contribution, and wanted it for himself. While not the decisive factor in attracting a great team of people, inner peace is so desperately wanted by so many people, that leaders who have it seem to attract the very best.

Azim Jamal says that a large part of his success in relationships has been his relaxed and easygoing nature: "I'm easy to get along with. I don't get too hyped about things. Small things don't worry me, and so people enjoy working with me." Jewelry designer Susan Rind says that her mentor, Ella Little, doesn't get worked up when things don't go as planned. Her commitment to making her boutique the best it can be outweighs disappointments; as seen in her calm and proactive response to challenges.

Being Non-Judgemental

Part of having inner peace is refraining from judging people. People who avoid judging others possess a calm demeanor and are much more likely to have strong relationships. Acceptance gives those around them freedom to act with confidence and harmony. Change consultant Rob McGregor explains his role in this process when working with clients: "I'm very conscious of building a safe environment, and that means letting go of judgement, because we all have radar out when we're in that 'blame and shame' place. We know when someone is measuring us, and we don't want to deal with that. So if I come in broadcasting that, there's no way they can find a way to move forward."

Moving forward is something many of the entrepreneurs talked about, particularly when two or more parties had opposing opinions or different agendas. Darren McDowell, of Just One Drop Water Shops, says that people like him because he "comes across in a way that is non-threatening," and this has influenced his ability to bring people to consensus. He says many individuals do not bother to understand others' points of view—one reason they fail to succeed in their personal or professional lives. John Maxwell, in *Winning With People,* emphasizes how common this problem is, saying: "Much of the conflict we experience in relationships comes from our failure to see things from the other person's perspective." Although this seems simple, most people don't act as though they value and understand it.

Refraining from judgement helps entrepreneurs learn from everyone. They learn what they want and what they don't want in business and life. They discover what they need to adapt and what will remain unchanged. Patti Fasan remembers a boss who was not admired by most people, but whom she learned bottom-line business skills from. Patti explains: "I didn't even like this individual, but when someone is so gifted at what they do, observe and find out why they are the way they are. As soon as you want to learn something from them, you tend to be less judgemental and a lot more open."

Consider This

▶ What does peace look like in your home? In your business?

▶ What can you do to have more peace at home and at work?

▶ If you practiced refraining from judgement, what
would that do for your business? For your life-
balance?

Clarity and Conciseness

All of the entrepreneurs I spoke with were exceptional
communicators—articulate and confident in their ability to
communicate verbally and non-verbally. Many of them
commented on the constant need for clarity in all parts of their
business. For example, some of the entrepreneurs regularly give
media interviews, and so the importance of giving clear, concise
information is crucial. Maureen Wilson of Sweat Co. studied
acting for years, and many of her present-day staff are also actors.
This led to a strong relationship with television crews, who
appreciated Maureen and her staff's ability to relate messages
in a clear, concise, and lively manner.

Brian Scudamore of 1-800-GOT-JUNK? says for years he
was the only PR person on his staff because he needed to clearly
understand his message before others could do so. His effectiveness
in clearly and concisely portraying the company's vision and business
practices gained him international attention, as people began
to take note of his franchise as a model for their own businesses.

Clarity and conciseness are also crucial in communicating
with employees. Laura Prosko, as an event management
professional, needs to be particularly careful about making sure
agreements for contract work are understood and that there are
no grey areas which could lead to either party's disappointment.
This clarity also serves herself and employees in not wasting
time because everyone knows exactly what is expected of them.
Wendee Lynn Cristante is also adamant about clarity, saying, "If
I was not understanding what you were asking me, I would tell
you to stop what you were doing and say in five words or less
what you want. That's how I live my life on a personal level,
because it's time consuming and I don't have a lot of time."
When communicating with other people, the *I Like You* Principle
can be damaged by not having clear intentions.

In *Trump: How to Get Rich*, Donald Trump lays down the law on ambiguity. He explains that equivocation, or using ambiguous words to conceal truth, is "an indication that you're unsure of yourself and what you're doing." Trump gives the example of one of his executives fence-sitting on a major decision, using ten minutes to say nothing about whether or not to go ahead with a project. When Trump asked him what he thought of the project in ten words or less, he said, "It stinks."

Consider This

▶ Is your communication with those connected to your business clear and concise? Can you think of times when lack of clarity resulted in business challenges? What one thing can you do to improve this skill and what impact would it have on your business?

Team Clarity: The Role of Technological Systems

Technology is used by most of the entrepreneurs to continually communicate goals, challenges and celebrations in a clear and efficient manner. Using shared technology such as Team Folders, owner John Stanton is able to coordinate the efforts of over one hundred employees. John says this creates a true team environment, where members can focus on what they need to do and see everyone else's work in progress, thereby, keeping the Big Picture in mind.

This use of technology for constant communication between team members has enabled the smooth, relatively problem-free openings of Running Room stores. John gives a recent example of opening three stores, all within a few weeks of each other, where twenty Team Folders were being worked on:

"You have to go in there and check to see each day that whatever you're responsible for has been dealt with. So now, when we open a store, we don't have to re-invent the whole formula because the formula is there. We know certain things have to happen. Here's what I do around the store opening, here's what the store set-up people do, here's what the area manager does, here's what the store manager does. It sounds silly, but pencils and toilet paper are those tasks. So you don't open a store and all of a sudden you discover you don't have toilet paper. Every store we open, those products arrive automatically."

John's point demonstrates the precision of the systems he has developed that allow his company to successfully manage rapid growth.

Clarity also develops when technology is used to free employees from distracting, time-consuming tasks. John ensures his managers across North America are focusing on what is most important and on what they do well:

"A lot of what you call traditional store management functions are done centrally. We centralized things like payroll and all the payables. We allow our people at the stores to do what's important, and that's looking after the customer. Our people are highly motivated. They're energetic. They're keen about talking about running and walking, and that's what we want them to do."

Being a Straight Shooter

Another aspect of communication connected to clarity is honesty and forthrightness. It sounds simple, yet can be difficult for entrepreneurs in times of conflict. Maureen Wilson is a role model of effective communication, as her employees see her as "tough but fair." She says, "If somebody was lying or inappropriate with clients then I would just be straight-up with them and say this isn't what we do here. And I try not to jump to conclusions when that happens, so they have a chance to talk to me and I to them."

Maureen's ability to deal with uncomfortable issues also puts new employees at ease, as they have the opportunity to talk about what they need financially. Again, Maureen stresses clarity in dealing with matters of money. "There's a very clear outline of what I'm getting and what they're getting. They know that they'll make a good living and that I'm fair to them." Money-talk can make some entrepreneurs nervous, but those that have the best relationships with employees address this issue, ensuring there are no mysteries that could lead to disillusioned employees.

Entrepreneurs also talked about honesty in selling and delivering their products and services. Sales experts say that trust is integral to the sale. It is no surprise that these entrepreneurs excel at bringing in and retaining clients. Their belief in the value of being forthright with everyone trickles down to employees as well. John Stanton, of the Running Room, trains his managers to be honest through his "three-way litmus test": "Is this a win for the customer, the Running Room and the community?" These questions help keep John's employees communicating in a direct and honest way.

Persuasiveness

Most of the entrepreneurs talked about their ability to be highly persuasive in order to accomplish a task or grow their business. Whether selling products and services, convincing someone to move halfway across the country to start a new business, or inspiring employees to reach a company vision or goals, the persuasive nature of these entrepreneurs was a distinct factor in their likeability quotient. Undeniably, people are attracted to those who are articulate, knowledgeable and passionate about their business and where it is headed, and don't mind being persuaded to do something *if* that something is in their best interest.

Persuasiveness is not always in what you say or how you say it—it is in honouring commitments and promises, doing what you say you will do, and doing the right thing, not always the easy thing. Trent Dyrsmid, when asked about how he managed to persuade a shareholder to give him $50,000 at a time when the company had not turned a profit for well over a year, said:

"I think that any successful entrepreneur, by their very nature, has to be persuasive, but persuasive not in the sense of slickster, snake-like salesman. Persuasive takes years to develop. Persuasive is about who you are, about your values, about your honesty, about your credibility, about what you've done in the past, about what you've said, about what you've followed through on."

Trent's relationship with his shareholder was one that developed over many years, and because Trent kept the Big Picture in mind, his "relationship account" was strong enough to endure difficult times.

The idea of a relationship account, similar to Stephen Covey's Emotional Bank Account metaphor, is useful in dealing with business associates or family. We can be persuasive with an individual only to the extent that our account with them is full. Azim Jamal talks about his relationship with his son, saying, "One thing that I learned from him is that I can't do any wrong with him because there's so much love; sometimes I get upset or angry and I feel bad and yet it doesn't even bother him because there's so much credit in the account. So what he's taught me is that if you invest that credit, if you invest it in a relationship, then a problem is no problem because there's so much good in the relationship." When Azim uses persuasive language with his son, there's a much higher likelihood that his son will consider his point of view.

Asking Questions

Everyone has a basic need to have their opinions matter. Even at a very young age, children who have the freedom to voice their opinions and have these opinions listened to, tend to be more self-confident as adults. Unfortunately, many adults hesitate to express opinions, and this is where the role of a leader can strengthen the *I Like You* Principle. People generally look forward to responding to questions that would make their work environment a more positive one for themselves and people around them. Laura Prosko talks about an event where she had

1200 volunteers, and asked for feedback from every one of them. Laura says, "I learn from the people I hire. Everybody has good ideas."

This willingness to learn more from the people around you not only makes good business sense, but endears you to employees. Ted Cawkwell says he has a close relationship with his employees, largely because he has a staff meeting every four days and asks for ideas to improve the lodge and for opinions on challenges: "If they have something to get off their chest or if they have ideas, I'm open to them and I almost always implement them. It's really great for them and it's really great for me, because I don't have to think of everything."

Brian Scudamore has systems in place where employees are constantly encouraged to share their opinions, from daily meetings to quarterly surveys. Posted on the company website are the top three things employees love about working for the company. The third most common response of over 100 employees was that the company respected and asked for the ideas and opinions of all employees. One employee wrote, "The fact that Brian and management care so much about OUR feedback and job satisfaction makes us all want to do our best to keep us on the path of achieving our goals." Not surprisingly, this franchise, in 2004 and 2005, was voted by Watson and Wyatt as the number one best company to work for in British Columbia.

Brian Scudamore also does something that very few CEO's do: he spends time talking and listening to employees on a regular basis. Brian even refuses to have his own office or desk. He "squats" with different departments, learning from them and helping them in pursuit of a common vision for the company. In *Tales from the Top*, Graham Alexander says that even today, he is still amazed by how many senior managers know nothing about the people they lead. Brian's interest in his team and the work they are doing, results in employee retention; with people feeling happier and motivated to meet personal and professional goals.

Listening

One of the relationship skills mentioned most often by entrepreneurs was that of being a good listener. Everyone responds well to someone skilled in the art of listening. Rob McGregor humorously illustrates this through a business experience. He was amongst leaders of a company who had a serious challenge to work through. They asked Rob's opinion of a question, and he remained silent, thinking of the best possible response to a dicey situation. As he remained silent, others began proposing solutions, and he acknowledged these with positive facial expressions, choosing to remain in listening-mode. At the end of the conversation, he hadn't uttered a word, yet the issue was resolved and everyone wanted him to coach the team. This story speaks well of the power of developing relationships through more silence, contemplation, and careful listening.

Rebecca Shafir, author of *The Zen of Listening*, says "A good listener sees himself as the receiver rather than the taker," adding, "It doesn't take a smart person to sense the difference between someone who listens in order to gain something and one who listens to build a relationship." George Preston listened to build relationships. Whether he was with the love of his life, wife Iris, or one of his employees at Preston Chev-Olds, listening was always a strength. During our interview, he asked me many questions about my life and my book, choosing to listen as much as he talked. Similarly, Ella Little and Laura Prosko asked about my business and referred me to potential clients. Months later, all of these entrepreneurs remembered minute details of our conversation. The *I Like You* Principle was in full force as their example reminded me how important listening is to improving existing relationships and forging new ones.

When entrepreneurs develop their listening skills, they are far more likely to fulfill and even exceed customer expectations. Ceramic Tile Consultant, Patti Fasan, says that when potential clients talk, she listens with every part of her body. She asks herself, "What is it that they need from me?" Because of her keen responsiveness to their needs, Patti is able to totally individualize programs. This skill has led her to receive countless referrals and testimonials that keep her business strong.

In *The Zen of Listening*, Rebecca Shafir recommends developing awareness of listening stoppers and listening encouragers. Listening stoppers are self-centered response styles that include denying others' perceptions of situations, attacking or criticizing through questions and giving unsolicited advice. She recommends replacing these annoying habits with listening encouragers, which are speaker-supportive styles that include silence, reassurance and paraphrasing.

Sam Walton was known as a listening leader, and used listening encouragers regularly. Touring Wal-Mart stores, he asked employees, including truckers and front-line people, for their best ideas. He also spoke directly to customers to discover their needs. By being inquisitive, yet respectful and non-threatening, Walton developed a speaker-supportive style that led to constant improvement of his company.

Caveat: Giving What We Don't Have Within

Alphonse Seward says his greatest skill is the ability to listen deeply. When I asked how he arrived at this level of listening, he told me that he has been developing the skill over the last fifteen years. Through unconventional men's retreats where he participated in drumming, singing, dancing and praying, he was able to examine different cultures, rituals and ways of creatively responding to emotions. Alphonse explains: "A lot of the listening that I wasn't practicing was the listening inside of me. I had to open up enough to let something new in."

When we don't listen to ourselves, we cannot use this gift to benefit the people in our lives. Often, our minds and bodies are so filled with our own troubles that it becomes difficult to help others. In turn, our relationships become weaker and the spiral effects of ineffective communication worsen. This impacts our business, as we cannot function effectively when primary love relationships are weak. Only when we give ourselves what we need, honouring our passions and values, can we give back to others.

Consider This

▶ Do you have the space to let others' words in? Do
you need to listen to yourself first? What can you
do to become a better listener?

▶ What traditional or unconventional methods
could you examine to reach a level of self-
awareness necessary to impact your listening
skills, thereby strengthening relationships?

▶ In networking situations, remind yourself that
part of good listening is asking questions that
show your interest in others. Questions that are
not intrusive, and start with "why", "what", or
"how", can be good conversation starters to learn
something and forge new relationships. Examples
may include: "What do you love about your new
business?", "What does the perfect client look like
in your business?" and "How do you find a
balance between work and home life?"

Wisdom in Action

It is the disease of not listening, the malady of not
marking, that I am troubled withal.

Shakespeare, King Henry the Fourth

The difference between a flower and a weed is ... a
judgement.

Susan Hayward

Write down three points of action you will take after reviewing this chapter. Then reflect on the quotes above and how these words translate to action in your life.

Chapter Ten

Surrounded by Good People

Much wisdom about the significance of strong relationships came from seasoned entrepreneurs. A common message was to surround yourself with good people—people who not only support your endeavours and share similar values, but who have reached exceptional levels of aptitude in areas you have not. By making strong connections and deeper relationships with these people, your personal and professional growth will heighten, not to mention happiness and enthusiasm! Business expert Jim Rohn says, "You are the average of the five people you spend the most time with." Other than mentors, who are mentioned in the next chapter, some or all of the following five groups significantly impact the entrepreneurs' business success:

▶ Life Partners

▶ Life/Business Partners

▶ Business Partners

▶ Employees

▶ Customers

Life Partners

Above all, people talked about their life partners as being crucial to their business success. The greatest form of this support came in their partner's attitude toward money and financial risk. Generally, if entrepreneurs' partners share the same philosophy of money and its role in their lives, the entrepreneurs are more motivated, confident, and happier to forge ahead despite tremendous challenges. This support kept some entrepreneurs from throwing in the towel in their early years of business.

John Stanton is one of them. He recalls a bleak time when bitterly cold weather almost destroyed his business. Just as the Running Room was beginning to grow, expanding locations and inventory, John watched his sales sink as the snowstorms and -35 Celsius temperatures kept even the most avid runners away. He remembers going home one day during this period and having his wife comment on his exhausted, anxious demeanor. Reaching into his pocket, he placed a dollar fifty-seven in front of his wife and said, "This is our wealth." Because the situation was so desperate the company would not make payroll that month, she agreed to sell her car, their only possession that didn't have a lien or liability. She then said something that changed John's perspective on business and life permanently:

> "What you have done with the Running Room has touched the lives of many people. We've made a difference. And if it doesn't make it, nobody will take that away from you. You've helped people overcome weight issues, you've helped people stop smoking, you've helped people dealing with a divorce or death or something in their lives, some sort of tragedy. You've helped people get a sense of community. And we've helped raise tons of money for various charities. And nobody can take that away from you. So if it doesn't work, we'll start all over again, the same as when we first got married. We had nothing, but we still had what's important in life."

Through memories of this conversation, John is reminded that what really counts are the values he contributes to, the level of enjoyment he brings to his work, and the impact he has on others. His wife's support of these values continues to influence John's business decisions, particularly around the reinvestment strategy that allows for quick expansion of the family-owned business. John explains that some entrepreneurial couples immediately spend money on luxuries, whereas he and his wife are more focused on expanding their business to make a difference.

Partners In Balance

Many of the male entrepreneurs relied on their partners to keep them balanced, particularly in the areas of mental and physical health. Professed workaholics, some of the men needed their partner's perspective to help them see when the scales tipped. From being "fed and watered" to being encouraged to participate in more family gatherings, to being asked to stop talking about business during family time, men acknowledged they have their partners to thank for being successful—particularly as popular notions of success move away from "who has the most" to "who has a full and balanced life".

While the above examples may seem stereotypical to some, the truth is, men and women offer their entrepreneurial partners equally valuable perspectives. Laura Prosko jokes that her mother and father respond in very different ways to her development as an entrepreneur. She tells her audiences, "My dad says, 'Live your dreams, do whatever you want to. Take on the world.' And my mom says, 'But wear your jacket. Did you eat first? Did you have a good breakfast?' " Laura's humorous story strikes a chord with her audiences because they recognize themselves or people they know in these roles. Dawn Garrick says when her husband came home from a day at All Weather Shelters, she needed to remind him of personal responsibilities like doctor appointments and his daughter's anniversary. Similarly, Mike Robinson of Ultra Span Structures says his wife provides him with balance by reminding him of when he is "disappearing into a corner and focusing on numbers". While this nurturing, practical side is one which is certainly not the sole domain of women, it is one which keeps many a busy entrepreneur from spiraling into health and relationship challenges.

Especially For Women

Women also spoke of the importance of a supportive partner, although not in the same context as men. For many of the women interviewed, the most important role their partners played was being consistently supportive of their business endeavours, showing full belief in their ability to tackle challenges and grow a successful business. Peri Shawn's husband, Tom Stoyan, has been her greatest cheerleader and inspiration as she took her coaching business from a part-time, after-work venture to a full-time, six-figure business. Because he is also a coach, the couple share perspectives on business philosophy, while respecting each other's differences.

Some women said their partners frequently expressed concerns over a lack of income, or were concerned when all the money earned was invested back into the business. These women noted that this tension between wanting to grow the business and providing a second income was not easy to deal with, and is one reason for the high rate of aborted businesses amongst women entrepreneurs.

▶ **My Story**

When I worked as a manager for a leading toy company, most of the successful women I had the privilege to learn from also had husbands who truly believed in their passion, commitment and ability to reach their goals. However, there were many more women who were constantly experiencing self-doubt despite successful business activity. This was in large part due to partners who saw the entrepreneurial venture as a hobby, until substantial income was flowing. Like these women, many others quit long before they realize their income goals; their significant others are not willing to forgo short-term financial gain for long-term business growth.

They do not share, or are not willing to wait for, the Big Picture that John Stanton's wife understood so well when all was at risk.

Conversely, I have seen couples who could have alleviated conflict by agreeing on what a successful business looks like financially in the first years. When beginning her consulting business, Patti Fasan had this discussion with her husband. He requested that she come up with a plan to earn "X" amount of dollars as an absolute minimum. She agreed, noting this money assisted with expenses but also demonstrated her commitment to the new business. Sometimes, if her consulting work wasn't bringing in the minimum, Patti creatively found ways to meet the financial goal. For example, she accepted interior design contracts while learning to market her business, become fluent with technology, and refine her speaking skills. Her willingness to go the extra mile led to her husband's increasing support of her business. He now refers to her as "The Wayne Gretzky of ceramic tile."

Consider This

▶ Check in with your loved ones about their true attitudes and thoughts about your business. If they could be more supportive, ask them why they feel the way they do about the business, and what you could do that would make them feel differently. Spousal support for entrepreneurs is imperative, and often, most important for women who have children and a partner, as statistically, they maintain the majority of responsibility in child care and home upkeep, while building their businesses.

▶ Come up with a financial plan with your partner. Setting a minimum, and even an achievable and extraordinary income goal, shows commitment and helps measure progress toward its attainment.

Life/Business Partners

Just as entrepreneurs appreciate their partners for offering different perspectives and keeping their lives balanced, so too do entrepreneurs who both work together and sleep together. Darren McDowell of Just One Drop Water Shops says he appreciates his wife Val's input and ideas in growing their business, while also acknowledging her nurturing role in keeping him healthy. Because the company's target market is primarily women with families, Darren appreciates Val's perspective. Val, however, grew into her role of providing ideas and feedback, as she initially envisioned handling only the administrative side of business. She admits that she left all the idea generating and problem solving up to her husband, until one day he confronted her, asking why she hadn't shared her ideas and opinions. Today, Darren and Val discuss ideas and challenges as a team.

Another benefit to doing business together is the variety of talents and skills couples bring to their businesses. Elana Rosenfeld of Kicking Horse Coffee says that she and husband, Leo, are a team with different talents: "We complement one another and we're a powerful, strong combination. I'm very organized and I pay attention to detail. And I'm very thoughtful and good at managing. Leo is very creative and loves change and loves new things, so he really pushes us forward."

Similarly, Farah Perelmuter of Speakers' Spotlight says her husband's background as a lawyer is very different from hers in advertising, but it's this difference that helped them survive in the early years of business and thrive today. "Martin is very focused and detail-oriented and extremely effective in sales. And I'm more the Big Picture and marketing. So, we complement each other. I think if we were both lawyers or both marketing people, we would not survive."

Farah also points out how having a partner is especially beneficial in times of challenge. She tells the story of organizing their first Speakers' Spotlight Showcase to benefit a children's charity, and discovering two weeks prior to the event that there were more speakers booked than clients registered! She says her husband was catatonic with stress, but she had the opposite reaction, putting herself into a wild frenzy. Martin helped Farah calm down while she boosted his energy level. By working together, they were able to have an incredible event packed with clients and considerable press coverage. The couple have since gone on to organize Showcase fundraisers annually for the past eleven years, raising hundreds of thousands of dollars to help better the lives of sick children.

While being business and life partners strengthens relationships in some ways, it also brings with it a unique set of challenges. Sandra Sereda says she and husband Murray often have different opinions about courses of action. She emphasizes, however, that the important thing is not whose decision is put into action, but rather, the overall respect that underlies discussions. Because of the couple's high regard for each other's opinions, a consensus is usually reached. On occasion, when debates become heated, Sandra reminds herself, "It's just a job. Don't worry about it." This attitude, along with mutual respect, has kept the couple together in business and life over the past two decades.

Elana Rosenfeld has been working with her husband, Leo, for over a decade, and says that while they have more in common and more to talk about, they have no break from each other. Avoiding business conversation during off-work times was particularly challenging for most of the entrepreneurial couples. Elana says sometimes two a.m. arrives and she and Leo are still talking business. Farah and Martin Perelmuter deal with this challenge by avoiding business talk at home after eight p.m. and on weekends. If they need to talk business, they make a point of doing it elsewhere.

For Dawn and Wally Garrick, however, the intention to set boundaries never happened. Although they both worked at their business, they rarely saw each other during business hours. This led to only one possible time and place to go over business matters—evenings at home. After several years of this practice and the combined stress of coping with household and family obligations, Dawn made a decision to step down from the company. She found her choice relieved personal and family stress. Her advice for entrepreneurial couples? Take steps necessary to keep business away from home, even if that means walking away from a particular role at work.

Another challenge, particularly for partners with a home-based business, is defining business roles. Rick and Jacqueline Jongkind have reached the pinnacle of success in a direct-sales company by being in the top one percent of income earners, yet they still have times when they struggle with their roles. Jacqueline explains that early on in their entrepreneurial ventures, Rick was away from home a lot, so when he made the transition to working full-time from home, she thought they could have discussions during the day, when others were at their job. Yet, Rick wanted to maintain the structure of set working hours where he didn't want to be interrupted. He says, "A lot of people struggle working from home. They just really get messed up with this whole thing. Because the roles get intertwined with one another, people don't really define what it is that they need to do." Rick was good at defining his roles in business, but needed to respond to his wife's needs. "I had to recognize that I'm not at an office anymore and I need to be flexible. So that was a work in progress. The toughest stuff we've gone through in our business has been that."

Consider This

▶ Whether you work with your spouse or not, how important is it to invest time in your role at home? What would be the value of ensuring business does not invade and engulf home life? What would help you keep home a priority?

▶ Schedule the amount of time you will work from home each day. Make sure it is realistic and in

keeping with your core values. If it isn't, what can
you do to change how you are working to meet
those values?

Business Partners

Many of the people interviewed were partners with at least one
other entrepreneur. **Like entrepreneurial couples, all of the
partners insisted that having access to each other's talents,
skills, and thought processes influenced their business
success.** Robert Murray, of MSM Transportation, Inc., echoes
this sentiment, saying, "I am a firm believer that you can take
two ideas from two individuals and what you get is much greater
than from each of those two minds. One plus one does not equal
two."

Many entrepreneurs viewed their partners' different
personalities as an asset. Often, one partner was perceived to
be more calm and reserved than the other, as in the case of *muzi
tea bar* owners, Brian Takeda and Mars Koo. Brian describes
Mars as analytical, objective, calm and rational. Conversely, Brian
is a born cheerleader and visionary, bringing excitement and
anticipation to daily decision-making. Brian admits, such vast
differences in personality can be challenging at times, but insists
that a balance of the opposites works out in their favour: "You
don't want someone to conclude that you're dreaming all the
time and have no sense of reality, like what I tend to do. And
then we have Mars on the other side of the spectrum. He's so
detailed and technical that I don't know if the company can
begin expanding and doing crazy things. So a nice average of
those skill sets is great."

Partners also complemented each other in managing Big
Picture or fine-detail skills. One of the two entrepreneurs was
often the creative visionary, whereas the other was able to execute
short-term goals in support of that vision. Trent Dyrsmid
demonstrates this when discussing the strengths of business
partner, Ed Anderson: "I think about where this business needs
to be in six months, but he runs it today." Ed's strengths in setting

up systems and managing systems and employees on a daily basis works well with Trent's ability to move the company forward with a clear sense of direction and an overall focus on the Big Picture.

In *What Happy Companies Know*, Dan Baker talks about the need for visionaries to pair themselves with operationally oriented people. He gives the example of Walt Disney, who was the artistic visionary, and brother Roy, who was the financial genius. Similarly, Sam Walton was Wal-Mart's visionary, and brother Bud excelled in operations.

Differences in partners is especially an asset in the early years of business, before delegation. Michael Gerber of *The E-Myth* says, "The typical business owner is only ten percent Entrepreneur, twenty percent Manager, and seventy percent Technician." This three-in-one role is problematic for many small-business owners, yet entrepreneurs I interviewed dealt with it by having partners who were more adept in certain roles than they were. Brian Takeda and Mars Koo, for example, quickly recognized their differing strengths to maximize business results, using Brian's creativity to develop novel tea product concepts, while relying on Mars' administrative and number crunching talents to make financial decisions.

Those who didn't have partners were adept in trading services with other professionals and eventually delegating when it became economically feasible. Often, this is not the case, as Jack Canfield points out in his book, *The Success Principles*. Lack of complete delegation, he believes, means that most entrepreneurs spend less than 30% of their time focusing on their strengths and unique abilities. This is one reason many companies fail to grow; owners cannot relinquish control over parts of their businesses, and spend much of their time doing tasks not suited to their strengths. Elana Rosenfeld says she recognizes this flaw in many small business owners, and advises entrepreneurs to be more aware of their tendencies to be excessively controlling. "You have to allow good people to come along in your organization and do a great job. You have to learn how to delegate and delegate well, and manage and manage well. But if you're trying to control the whole thing, you're never going to get anywhere."

Consider This

▶ Mike Robinson says that both his wife and business partner are very different from him, and reminds entrepreneurs that, "It's easy to get into a relationship with people who are the same as yourself, and then you tend to get advice from people who are the same as yourself, which is not necessarily the best thing." Prolific author and psychologist Wayne Dyer says that most of us seek out partners and friends based on similarities, without ever taking steps to value diversity of thought, behaviour and personality.

▶ If you don't already have a business partner, what differences would you value in acquiring a partner? What three differences would most likely lead to company growth and personal growth on your part?

Employees: An Examination of 1-800-GOT-JUNK?

For many entrepreneurs, being surrounded by great employees is a big part of their success—even bigger than having a clear vision. This is fully supported by research done in Jim Collins' book, *Good To Great*. One of Collins' most significant findings was that good to great companies first get the right people on the bus (and the wrong people off the bus) before they figure out where to drive it. He illustrates this with the actions of Dick Cooley, the CEO of Wells Fargo in the early '70's. Cooley knew the banking industry was to undergo dramatic change but didn't know exactly what shape that change would take, so he hired the most outstanding people he could find, often without a particular job in mind, believing they would adapt. Cooley was right. During a time when that particular banking industry fell far behind the general stock market, Wells Fargo outperformed the market more than three times. Astonishingly, Collins reported that nearly every person hired went on to become a CEO of a major company. The right people on the right bus can and do take companies from average to outstanding.

One CEO took his company from good to great, and is an adamant supporter of hiring the right people. When asked what he did to encourage a positive culture, his response was: "finding the right people." Brian Scudamore of 1-800-GOT-JUNK? says, "We make sure we recruit the right people because I don't think you can motivate people. I think you can only find motivated people. So we're finding people here that want to have fun, that want to be part of an energetic culture, that already possess those traits." Similarly, Milton Lake Lodge owner, Ted Cawkwell, talks about hiring people for his fishing lodge based on their passion to be there, a practice many naysayers warned would be the death of his business. However, Ted hasn't regretted his decision, saying, "I've got a terrific group of people who are gung ho and loyal to the same vision as me. My vision can't rub off on someone, so looking for people with the same passion and sharing of a vision is important."

So Now That You Have Them, How Do You Keep Them?

Brian Scudamore is a leader in employee retention. There are several things his team does well when it comes to retaining employees. Firstly, they focus on bringing the "right" people on the bus, ensuring they are all in the "right" seats. The most important part of treating individuals right, he explains, is simply ensuring they are a strong cultural fit for the company: highly energetic, positive, and passionate about their work and the company's vision. When people work with others who have these same qualities, work becomes fun—a place where people look forward to spending time. Brian says that he loves going to work every day because he gets to be around people who exude these qualities.

Brian's employees are also quick to point to their love for the people that surround them at work. Employee, Carolyn Mackinnon, says "The people here rock. They are all considerate, intelligent and a lot of fun to work with." Andrea Baxter says, "I love that after almost being here for one year, it still doesn't feel like a job," and Amelia Barker says, "The energy and enthusiasm of the people working here makes it a real pleasure to be part of the team." These findings parallel the research of *Good to Great* author, Jim Collins, who reports that the people he interviewed from good-to-great companies loved what they did, mostly because they loved who they did it with.

The people who contribute to this fun culture separate 1-800-GOT-JUNK? from other large franchises and corporations, which operate under tense and oppressive atmospheres. In surveys and interviews posted on the company's website, employees recognize their own contribution to the culture, while simultaneously celebrating the leaders who help envision it. Whether it be the addition of Brian's dog Grizzly as "one of the gang", their Blue Wigs branding campaign, or the daily Huddle, when achievements of employees and franchisees are celebrated, the central office is humming with fun and excitement. Employee, Jillian Wong, says, "I love the team spirit that I get when I walk into the office. Everyone gets along and spirits are high. It makes coming here not 'just a job'. It's a chance to also see friends, have laughs, and generally have a great time at work." Again, finding the right group of people is more than just getting the best candidate for a particular job. The right people create an energy that synthesizes into an unstoppable, dynamic team.

You may be thinking, "But are they productive?" With over 70 million in sales in 2005, and strong progress to reach a goal of 100 million by the end of 2006, it's clear that a fun environment is not only possible in a high-growth company like 1-800-GOT-JUNK?, but vital to its stability.

Freedom and Trust Matter

Brian Scudamore's employees lauded freedom as a reason for loving their workplace. Many people appreciate the flexible scheduling which allows them to effectively meet the demands of their personal and professional lives. Brian explains:

> "If someone doesn't want to come in one day and needs to work from home, great. They know what needs to get done and we're holding them accountable to the job they've got to get done. And we're trusting people. We're saying 'Listen, you've got a job to do, do it. How you get it done doesn't really matter, as long as you're consistent with our values.'"

This demonstration of basic trust with accountability is something many employees commented on, as it's not commonly practiced in organizations. Employee, Lori Mae McCullough, says, "There is a great deal of trust in our organization. It is a breath of fresh air to work without having someone constantly looking over your shoulder. We are viewed as trustworthy, mature professionals and treated accordingly."

1-800-GOT-JUNK? has minimized social hierarchy, which also adds to a sense of trust, equality and freedom. Even as CEO of a 100 million dollar company, Brian Scudamore does not believe in the glass tower approach, and does not have his own office or desk. Instead, he "squats" amongst different departments, learning from his team, and asking questions crucial to company growth, much like Wal-Mart's legendary leader, Sam Walton. Brian even asks for employee input on the hiring of people they will work closely with. Such actions have made Brian's company a model for others, who struggle with employee satisfaction and stress levels. In *What Happy Companies Know*, Dan Baker says stress is related to social hierarchy, citing Michael Marmot's *The Status Syndrome*: "Social Hierarchy signifies how much control you feel over your life and that this sense of control is directly related to disease." 1-800-GOT-JUNK? employees appreciate the minimized hierarchy and maximized personal control, no doubt leading to a happier and healthier workplace.

Avoid Micromanagement

Many entrepreneurs talked about the importance of trusting employees. By observing others who are over-controlling, Elana Rosenfeld learned that micromanaging never leads to strong business growth. She explains that knowing who you are and what your talents and skills are is critical, allowing you to focus on strengths while others focus on theirs. Ken Funk, former president of Golden Valley Foods, also says that giving employees the opportunity to do their jobs has been integral to his company's success. Effective management, he notes, is crucial— management that holds people responsible for their actions, but gives them the freedom to be creative and get things accomplished with their unique talents.

In talking to Kristy Cantin, a friend who works for a successful entrepreneurial couple, I discovered that employees may need to be guided in order to do an effective job, but the right people don't want to be spoon-fed. They enjoy having ownership over daily decisions that make a difference to the success of the company. Kristy says she is motivated to go to work because she knows her creativity flourishes in a company where she is encouraged to develop new ideas or adjust existing practices.

Eric Huang says one reason he became an entrepreneur was because of a distinct lack of such opportunities as an employee. If you examine the website of 1-800-GOT-JUNK?, many employees extol the virtues of their management team, who give opportunities for advancement. Why don't more companies who find the right people let the right people help them grow the business? Asking ourselves why we have certain negative or counter-productive tendencies, and doing something about these tendencies, is critical to business success.

Does Money Matter?

Entrepreneurs agree that people need to be paid fairly. Some did regular surveys to ensure employees were satisfied with their wages, among other work-related conditions. Eric Huang says some employees seek not only a certain level of pay, but stability of income. If they know, for example, that the company has a good reputation and has been around for several years, they are more likely to want to stay.

Entrepreneurs also said there needs to be some perks for performance. In the call centre of 1-800-GOT-JUNK?, many employees are young students, who usually don't have their own transportation, so one of the perks for the highest bi-monthly sales is driving a Mini with the company's logo boldly displayed. A costly incentive for some business owners, but great advertising. The company's generous vacation pay of five weeks is also a big perk.

Despite these two great company incentives, 1-800-GOT-JUNK? employees rarely list these as top reasons for loving the company, which begs the question, what does make employees stay? Again, admiration and respect for the people they work with, as well as the fun culture and commitment to values, rate highest. But in the retail industry, where wages are typically low unless you are in upper management, what other incentives are there for people to stay? Running Room owner John Stanton says that because he hires those passionate about running, it is their love of the sport that often persuades them to stay. This thread of passion is a common denominator among employees of many successful companies.

From single business-fronts like Ella's boutique to large franchises like 1-800-GOT-JUNK?, front-line people have a passion for either the product or the business vision, and often, both. Ella Little's employees love beautiful, high quality designer clothing and are passionate about creating stunning displays or finding the perfect outfit for their customers. Harvey McKinnon's employees are passionate about helping non-profits achieve their goals, since they believe in social responsibility and social justice. Call-centre employees at 1-800-GOT-JUNK? are passionate about the company's vision and how their role influences the outcome of that vision. This level of excitement, when shared by a large group of people, inevitably contributes to lower staff turnover rates and fewer sick days.

Personal recognition of employees is also something many of the companies engaged in on a consistent basis. Again, Scudamore is a leader in this category, as he ensures every day, during the staff Huddle, there is time for celebration of someone. In the Huddle, people cheer as they recognize personal events and accomplishments like birthdays and charitable initiatives. Franchisees all over North America are recognized for reaching their goals, and everyone applauds progress toward the company goal. Because Scudamore blends life and business in a brief but boisterous celebration, he keeps employees' spirits high, and this atmosphere carries through into the rest of the day.

Customers: Craving Consistency

One of the great benefits to having daily meetings like the Huddle is that people have a deep inherent need for basic structure and consistency. Even as young children, those who have morning and evening routines grow up more grounded and have less behavioural challenges. Children who play musical instruments do best when they practice daily at the same time and for the same length of time. This positive human response to basic routines or systems transfers well to the world of work, as seen in the Huddle. People not only are excited to share victories and positive news regularly, but also feel a sense of stability in knowing they are listened to.

Several of the entrepreneurs interviewed talked about the need for consistency not only within their companies, but with their customers and clients. John Stanton demonstrates this in his Running Room stores across North America in several ways. Year-round Wednesday evening and Sunday morning running clinics provide comfort and familiarity to a transient population. Because these clinics are free, newcomers don't need to worry about extra costs. In Canadian Running Room stores, there is a set price for products, no matter if a customer is looking for the same pair of runners in St. John's, Newfoundland or in Vancouver, British Columbia. Remote locations, regardless of exorbitant shipping costs, have identical pricing to all other Running Room locations. This consistency is critical to customer trust, and even automobile companies like Toyota have implemented a consistent pricing policy, regardless of location.

A final, and perhaps, most significant point, is that because John hires people who have a passion for running, they can relate to the experiences of most customers. He notes that although each store has its own personality, the constant is that customers are served by well-informed, energetic, motivated people, who share their passion for the sport. This consistency also plays out in the atmosphere of the Running Room, where the small and intimate surroundings make people feel at home. And for many runners, it is home. Loyal customers come in several times a week, sometimes seeking the companionship of fellow runners, sometimes a motivational lift from employees.

Wisdom in Action

How much finer things are in composition than alone.

Ralph Waldo Emerson

Perhaps the clearest and deepest meaning of brotherhood is the ability to imagine yourself in the other person's position, and then treat that person as if you were him. This form of brotherhood takes a lot of imagination, a great deal of sympathy, and a tremendous amount of understanding.

Obert C. Tanner

Write down three points of action you will take after reviewing this chapter. Then reflect on the quotes above and how these words translate to action in your life.

Chapter Eleven

Seek and You Shall Find: Mentors for Business, Mentors for Life

Azim Jamal's reminder to be open to learning from others is wisdom put into action by all the entrepreneurs. There were, however, significant differences in how these business people viewed and approached the subject of mentoring. While the great majority insisted mentoring was vital to their success, their views on the structure and type of mentoring differed. Generally, entrepreneurs promoted three "schools" of mentorship:

▶ Long-Term Mentors

▶ Short-Term Mentors

▶ Formal Mentoring Groups

Long-Term Mentors

Some of the entrepreneurs talked about business mentors who had been with them for several years, and in some cases, decades. Peter Legge often talks and writes about three business leaders who became his mentors: Ray Addington, Mel Cooper and Joe

Segal. In his book, *The Runway of Life*, Peter says that his relationship with these three men evolved over the past four decades to such an extent that their advice and influence became invaluable. He quotes Lord Chesterfield when advising others to form similar relationships: "We are more than fifty per cent of who and what we are, based on the role models that we pick. Therefore, it is important to be very careful which models we choose."

Legendary entrepreneur, Joe Segal, remains the most influential role model in Peter's life. Peter met Joe in his early twenties while selling radio advertising. Every few weeks, he would stop at Joe's office to make a pitch for an advertising spot. While Joe refused every time, Peter kept coming, increasingly interested in becoming friends with, and learning from, the incredible philanthropist and business leader. Peter eventually left the radio station, but began having regular lunches with Joe at the Four Seasons Hotel. He notes, in *The Runway of Life*, that he would sometimes just sit and listen to Joe talk about his life and the gems of wisdom from his experiences.

It was during one such visit that Peter came up with his concept for *The Runway of Life*. Joe explained that life is not a highway or a road, as many perceive it to be, but, "more like a runway—because at some point you're going to run out of asphalt." Peter used this metaphor in his keynotes to thousands of people monthly, challenging them with the question, "How much time are you willing to waste?"

While Peter's initial persistence in developing a relationship with Joe Segal paid off, he points out that mentors often choose us as much as we choose them. This was the case for Wally Garrick, whose loyal customer from a failed business became his mentor. When Wally began developing All Weather Shelters, his mentor, a retired businessman, saw Wally's drive and ability and began inviting him to his home and on fishing trips. During these visits, Wally's mentor asked questions and listened carefully to dilemmas and challenges, but never directly answered questions. Wally notes that this is important in a mentor, advising entrepreneurs to look for a sounding board—someone who will allow you to grow by guiding you through decisions rather than supplying the answer.

Qualities of Mentors

Wally's description of his mentor's traits can be found in many effective mentors. The ability to listen carefully and ask the right questions are crucial to the mentoring process. **Despite the fact that most people want answers immediately, it is the questions that prove to be invaluable in the long run.**

Effective mentorship also involves finding a mentor who has nothing to lose or gain by taking on this role. Wally notes that, ideally, a mentor is someone not emotionally involved with the business, yet understands your challenges because he or she has been in similar situations.

Entrepreneurs also described their mentors as being honest, tell-it-like-it-is communicators. The mentors were, without exception, willing to risk being "pals" so the entrepreneurs could more clearly understand themselves and their businesses. Susan Rind says her mentor, Ella Little, gave her the courage to continue developing her business despite adversity. But not through stroking and coddling. Rather, Ella took the "tough love" approach and told Susan to get over the rejection, pick herself up, and move on. While many people look for mentors who can sympathize with personal challenges, what they often need is the honest evaluation of that challenge by someone outside of their own business. Susan didn't need a "poor you, isn't that awful" response as much as she needed to hear that rejection is part of business and that choosing to move forward is necessary.

Eric Huang was grateful to have a straight-shooting mentor when first immigrating to the U.S. from China. Although he had reached celebrity status as a business consultant for the Chinese government, he was almost fired from his first job in a Texas food retailer chain due to cultural differences. His mentor, a general manager for a manufacturing plant, helped him to adjust to the aggressive and competitive nature of business in America. This helped him openly display his confidence and abilities.

The last, and most crucial trait entrepreneurs value in mentors, is integrity and general strength of character. Too often, people seek long-term mentors based solely on a history of financial success. All of the long-term mentors, however, were valued more for their ability to follow through on commitments and act according to their highest values. As Ozzie Jurock says of his three long-term mentors, "They were doers. They weren't just talking about it. So many times you have visionaries that get you motivated, but then you look at their life and it's not really there."

Consider This

▶ What qualities do you deem necessary in an ideal mentor? What basic values would this mentor uphold? Set an intention to find a mentor like this and begin taking small daily actions towards making this intention a reality. Some examples might be attending more networking events, praying and meditating, and journaling, not only to get clear on how a mentor can help you, but what you can do for your mentor. Peter Legge says, "You need to give back to your mentors as much as they give to you, because they're going to give you the most precious thing they've got, which is time on their runway. And your responsibility is to lead a life that they can be proud of."

Short Term Mentoring: Ask and Observe

Another group of entrepreneurs preferred to have short-term mentors, or helpful individuals that mentor in a very specific area of business or life. Brian Scudamore and Trent Dyrsmid, both in their mid-thirties, call on individuals they consider successful in the areas they are seeking help. Brian says his search for specific mentors has led him to be advised by the best of the best, including the former CEO of Monster.com, and a top executive of Subway. He seeks to learn from a variety of companies because he believes no company can do everything well, but many companies do specific things with greatness. Trent Dyrsmid, in beginning a second business, called the founders of several Internet companies and asked if they'd be willing to share their expertise on creating Internet businesses. The response he received was so detailed that he was immediately able to implement their advice.

In the search for short-term mentors, entrepreneurs become keenly aware of the everyday teachings of those around them. Rick Jongkind says, "You never know where they're going to come from, and they may not even be your business partners. There are times when I needed real help on the spiritual side of my life and somebody popped up who was a spiritual mentor at the time, and you get fed what you need to be fed for that period of time."

Azim Jamal agrees with the practice of learning from many people, saying, "People have different strengths. If you become a know-it-all, you never have any mentors. You think you are the mentor." He cites the example of his parents, wife and children as being mentors in his life, saying they have strengths he learns from daily. Azim regularly quotes his son in his inspirational newsletter along with the great sages and business people of history. One of his favorite words of wisdom from his son is: "An ounce of listening is better than a pound of talking." Listening to everyone, whether they are our family or the Donald Trumps of business, is more effective than being the business owner who wants only to be heard.

Consider This

▶ Are you directly and indirectly seeking the short-term guidance necessary for business growth and self-growth? How can you become more informed and aware of opportunities to do so?

The Power of Observation

Rick and Azim's advice can be seen in the awareness and observations made by many of the other entrepreneurs interviewed. Ken Funk and Susan Rind went on business trips with their mentors to simply observe. As a former teacher, Ken knew nothing about growing his jam business, and gladly accepted invitations to go on sales trips with a highly skilled businessman. His trips involved going directly into buyers' offices with his mentor to learn about basic sales programs, like a "deal of the month". Ken chuckles as he recalls having no idea what a deal of the month was. His tremendous gratitude towards his mentor at that time is evident, referring to him as his "angel".

Susan Rind's invitation to go on purchasing trips to New York with her mentor, Ella Little, helped her discover her own sense of style. Susan saw, first-hand, the latest top designer creations and how they were displayed. When she pulled out her camera, Ella refused to let her photograph, saying, "No, you have a creative eye. Take notes, go home, and develop your own style." This insistence on observation is what led Susan to her own unique style and to the subsequent value of her jewelry.

Many entrepreneurs talked about values gleaned through careful observation of their mentors. Sandra Sereda, owner of multiple businesses, recalls two former employers who gave her enormous freedom to initiate and follow through on ideas and concepts. When it came time to own her own business, she was adamant that her employees also have this same opportunity for ownership and advancement. Speakers, Peter Legge and Azim Jamal, saw their families as significant mentors in their lives; both, witness to the generosity of their parents, who gave regularly of their time, resources and wisdom, helping their community and those less advantaged. Not surprisingly, Azim and Peter are well-known for their philanthropy, continuing their parents' legacy.

Formal Mentoring Groups

Some entrepreneurs took action to create their own partnership with a group of people who would mentor each other. These groups offered participants a chance to celebrate victories, discuss challenges, and listen to the advice and opinions of others. Ozzie Jurock formed a group that he knew would be beneficial to many. Formed in the late '90's, it focused on managing massive restructuring in the real estate industry. The group consisted of senior executives who had lain off huge numbers of middle management. "Nobody was talking to anyone anymore. We were in the mode of downsizing, and so we had a mentor club where like-minded people could get together."

In *Networking Magic*, Rick Frishman and Jill Lublin talk about the success of a group similar to those Ozzie and Rick created. The Hubbel Group was a women's group, which began when a remarkable woman, Julia Hubbel, experienced a series of personal and professional tragedies in a short time. Because she moved to a new area and, like Ozzie, saw the need for a supportive and purposeful gathering, she formed a small and intimate group that met monthly. The structure of these meetings included four criteria: each woman would tell the group what she was best at, what she wanted to celebrate, what updates or news occurred since the previous meeting that would be of interest to the members, and what she needed help with. Frishman and Lublin note that requests for help were often the most difficult aspect of the meeting, as many women were not comfortable doing this. Yet, as entrepreneur Rick Jongkind notes, these requests are okay, and essential to business growth.

Consider This

▶ Develop your own mentor group. Who will be invited? What will the structure of the group look like? What rules will be put in place to benefit everyone equally? For an excellent guide to creating and maintaining such a group, please read *One Circle—Tapping the Power of Those Who Know You Best* by Maureen Fitzgerald.

Wisdom in Action

"Be mindful of who great teachers are."

Patti Fasan

Entrepreneurs do not need to know all the answers. All they need to know is who to call.

Robert Kiyosaki, Rich Dad's Before You Quit Your Job

Write down three points of action you will take after reviewing this chapter. Then reflect on the quotes above and how these words translate to action in your life.

Chapter Twelve

Networking and Alternatives that Work

Just as mentors and mentoring groups are important to many entrepreneurs, so too, is networking. While some people avoid networking because they dread conjuring up unauthentic "chit-chat", the truth is that successful business people see networking as much more than a casual, one-time meeting of strangers. They are inclined to view it as an opportunity to build strong relationships and valuable long-term connections. By having this perspective, entrepreneurs are well-received and respected by acquaintances.

Most entrepreneurs interviewed advised others to set a goal of networking to build meaningful connections. They also suggested tips to reach this goal and other business aspirations. These include:

▶ Clarifying and Stating Intentions

▶ Helping Others

▶ Gathering Referrals

▶ Researching Networking Alternatives

Clarifying and Stating Intentions

Like Rick Jongkind and the Hubbel Group, one of the keys to making networking effective is being clear about the help you need and asking for it. Laura Prosko regularly met with a high profile friend in politics, but had never shared her goal involving a prospective television project for women in business. One day, over a cup of coffee, Laura hesitantly told him about it, and was met with an enthusiastic response, as he happened to know people that could assist her. Laura was hooked up with experts in the film and television industry whom she never would have had access to otherwise.

Letting your intentions be known is also something Brian Scudamore practices, in both systematic and unstructured ways. At his head office in downtown Vancouver, Scudamore has devoted an entire wall to the goals and intentions for 1-800-GOT JUNK? The title on the wall is "Can You Imagine", and can be seen by every visitor and employee of the company daily. The goals, painted on the wall and check marked when achieved, come from Brian and his team of employees and franchisees. One such dream was to be featured on a Starbucks mug with a quote about removing the junk in our lives. When one of hundreds of franchisees saw this goal on the wall, he told Scudamore that he knew the project manager responsible for finding Starbucks quotes. As a result, Scudamore is soon going to have his company name and wisdom in the hands of coffee drinkers across North America.

Helping Others

Another focal point of making networking work is to be genuinely interested in helping others, and to take that extra step to be known for that. Laura Prosko illustrates this concept with her wide network of friends and acquaintances. When I asked her how she managed, as a novice comedian, to get gigs in New York, she revealed that ten years ago she had helped a co-worker to succeed, and now this same woman convinced her own agent to fly Laura out to perform. Laura says, that regardless of time passed, "When you help someone it comes back full-circle."

Because Laura and many other entrepreneurs believe in the power of assisting others in need, they see networking not as a series of transactions, but as a long-term process, where the entrepreneur and their business become a pillar in the community. Terry Smith talks about community and how it impacts business:

> "This is my seventh year as a town councilor, but I was very involved even before that as President of the Downtown Merchants Association and as the Director for the Langley Chamber of Commerce. So I've always been involved with the community and I think that's part of networking. You need to know people in your community if you're going to have a business in the community. I've always been amazed at people who open a business, open the doors, and just expect people to rush in. It just doesn't happen that way."

Peter Legge developed his wide network by following in his father's footsteps. Bernie Legge, an avid volunteer and pillar in his New Westminster community, always told Peter, "You need to give back to the community infinitely more than you take out." Inspired by his father's example, Peter spearheaded many national and international fundraising efforts, such as an $850,000 fundraiser to provide hope for Rwandans who survived genocide. From his work as an emcee for the annual Variety Telethon, that has now raised over 120 million, to his work with local charitable groups like Vancouver's Salvation Army, Peter has brought hope to thousands of people.

While making dreams come true for others, Peter befriended many individuals he might not have otherwise met. This list includes world leaders, athletes, and even royalty. In *The Runway of Life*, he tells of going to a Variety International Convention, due to his work with the organization, and being introduced to Princess Michael of Kent, who had a passion for books and had written her own biography. When she discovered Peter was also an author and in the publishing industry, she invited him for lunch at Kensington Palace. In turn, Peter hosted a lunch in Vancouver for Prince Michael, a cousin to the Queen, who was promoting Britain's small business sector. Because of these connections with the royal couple, he was asked to invite them to attend the opening night of the refurbished Queen Elizabeth Theatre in downtown Vancouver. Peter's story illustrates two valuable points for entrepreneurs: First, getting involved in your community often leads to strong networking connections where you learn from others and experience opportunities. Secondly, having something to offer people from all walks of life can, and often does, result in new and wonderful insights and experiences.

Consider This

▶ Make a list of what you have to offer people. Do you have a wide network of friends and acquaintances? Do you have knowledge of a particular industry that could be useful to others? Does your knowledge of current events, statistics or even everyday experiences come in handy during conversation? What passions do you likely share with others?

▶ If volunteering is something you would consider, what focused efforts, using your greatest talents and skills, could make a difference to groups of people? Have you met other volunteers you can learn from, both in a business capacity and as a leader in life?

Gathering Referrals

A third point about effective networking, is that viewing yourself and your business through the microscopic lens of others will let you know whether people want to do business with you. Do your words or actions demonstrate strength of character, such as integrity, commitment and respect? Does your business deliver high quality, competitively priced products and services? Would others want to refer you, based on that level of customer service? Taking the time to examine these questions weekly ensures that your networking efforts produce the results you want, namely, word of mouth referrals and connections to other business people who could assist you, and you, them.

Even celebrities choose products and services based on word-of-mouth. Just ask Maureen Wilson of Sweat Co. From NHL players, to musicians and actors like Michael Buble and Alicia Silverstone, Sweat Co. continually attracts superstars. Maureen insists she hasn't done anything magical to attract these dynamos—just provides a relaxed, intimate atmosphere where employees are instructed to avoid contacting press or creating their own celebrity hype. She is continually amazed by the power of referrals, saying, "I always shake my head about that because one person knows another person and then all these people from L.A. know us." Of course, Maureen's success with celebrities developed over time, but the fact that it happened at all, points again to the constants of receiving referrals and continuously providing quality products and services.

Ozzie Jurock teaches others about the power of referrals. He believes that in order to be successful in business, you need to have thirty relationships with professionals who are willing to provide new sources of referrals for you: "If you have thirty people who know what you do, that like what you do, and that like you, and are professionals in the market place, they're your pillars on which you build everything else." Ozzie explains that most people spend a fortune using personal items like pens, paper and calendars to promote themselves, when what they need to concentrate on is personal promotion, or building the relationships that will result in referrals.

Ozzie's advice to all entrepreneurs is to take action to develop relationships with thirty Professional Pillars who will not only be a source of referrals, but may also become your advisory board. He gives the example of having a local alderman and a lawyer as two possibilities on your "board", and notes that in order for this to be effective, several steps need to be taken: "You have to explain to them what you do, you have to meet with them on a regular basis, you have to send them information, and you have to reward them." Ozzie rewards his group with helpful newsletters and information specific to their industry, on a quarterly basis. This not only reinforces the giving relationship required in successful networking, but also keeps him continually in the minds of the people most likely to give referrals or advise him on business matters.

Marketing expert Wendy McClelland uses a similar success strategy by delivering tremendous value to her clients even after their contract is complete. Wendy explains: "I try to be my clients' own personal Google. I try to find resources and always send them things. These clients refer me to other people."

Researching Networking Alternatives

While networking has helped many people grow their businesses and develop strong relationships, traditional networking models do not work for everyone. For instance, some groups encourage people to introduce themselves to as many people as they can in a brief timeframe, telling others what they do and passing along a business card. Maureen Fitzgerald, president of CenterPoint Inc., says that such activities often don't result in referrals because: "It's human nature that I'm not going to refer you unless I know you. And I'm not going to help someone unless I know them. I have a big pet peeve with the whole networking model. I don't have a coffee and then refer you. I have a coffee, then I have an e-mail, then I have another coffee, then I go for lunch with you, and then I might mention it, but it's not just going to happen immediately." Maureen knows many business people who also felt strongly about making deeper connections in ways that encourage community building. Consequently, she now helps corporations and entrepreneurs develop their own groups, called Circles, and has written two books about creating and sustaining Circles.

In *One Circle—Tapping the Power of Those Who Know You Best*, Maureen describes a Circle as a "group of like-minded people helping each other be their best." Maureen explains that not only do the Circle members help each other achieve their goals and live meaningful lives, but they are also given greater opportunities to solve problems and live a life of balance. Over time, Maureen explains, the Circle strengthens, as trusting and supportive relationships create both "a safe place to have candid conversations" and "a connected community and inviting space where members feel open to sharing stories, experiences, and advice." **In a world where people are craving a sense of connection and community, Circles can be a welcome alternative to traditional networking.**

Consider This

▶ What forms of networking or alternatives to traditional networking speak to you? Do the results of your current networking meet your personal and professional goals? If not, what steps can you take to meet these goals?

Wisdom in Action

A single conversation with a wise man is better than ten years of study.

Chinese Proverb

The fragrance of what you give away stays with you.

Earl Allen

Write down three points of action you will take after reviewing this chapter. Then reflect on the quotes above and how these words translate to action in your life.

Final Thoughts

A few months ago I was halfway through a run when the usual challenge hit me: laboured breath, lead legs, and a strong desire to walk back home. Having exercised regularly for years, I knew this familiar challenge, yet never had a plan of action to deal with it. That day, I made a decision to do something about it. I went to the local Running Room and picked up John Stanton's book, *Running: Start to Finish*. I didn't even have to open it. Looking at the runners' physiques on the front cover was all I needed—shoulders back, chest out and head up. Of course! I wasn't getting enough air. My body simply needed to let it in. Basic breathing became much easier when I pulled my slouching shoulders back and lifted my chin, allowing my airways to open and shifting my focus on the horizon.

To this day, I am continually amazed by how seemingly insignificant adjustments, whether physical, emotional, mental or spiritual, make a big difference in people's lives. The stories and strategies within this book are specific, practical, start-today tools that lead to that difference. Tools to strengthen self-belief and add clarity to future plans and present focus are crucial in sculpting the business body. Improving relationship skills and defining systems adds definition to the sculpture, allowing the beauty and form of your business to come forth.

Small, focused actions bring me back to the wisdom of Malcolm Gladwell's *The Tipping Point*, which illustrates that ordinary people have the power to create large-scale change he labels "social epidemics". Gladwell explains: "Merely by manipulating the size of a group, we can dramatically improve its receptivity to new ideas. By tinkering with the presentation of information, we can significantly improve its stickiness. Simply by finding and reaching those few special people who hold so much social power, we can shape the course of social epidemics." In much the same way, you too can take small actions that have the power to create significant results. It is my hope that the sculpting stories and strategies in this book help you reach a "tipping point" in both your self-growth and business success.

Biographies

Brenda Alberts

The owner of Birthplace of B.C. Gallery, Brenda Alberts has a passion for art and is dedicated to the promotion of talented local British Columbian artists. Her commitment to these artists and her community has seen her win the 2004 Paul Harris Fellow Award from Rotary International, Business of the Year award by the Township of Langley Chamber of Commerce, and a nomination for the Arts Excellence award at B.C.'s Women of Excellence, 2000. Birthplace of B.C. Gallery celebrated its tenth anniversary in September, 2006.

Ted Cawkwell

Ted Cawkwell is the owner and president of Milton Lake Lodge, a luxury fishing lodge located in remote northern Saskatchewan. Ted was awarded Rookie Business of the Year by Saskatchewan Tourism for the best new tourism business in 2006, and won the same award a few years earlier for Ice Dreams Canadian Winter Adventures. This recognition has resulted in two major television shows featuring Milton Lake Lodge. Ted has also been featured in *Outdoor Canada* magazine's front cover and Canadian

Tourism dubbed his lodge one of the leading luxury lodges in Canada.

Wendee Lynn Cristante

Since 2001, Wendee Lynn Cristante's Canadian Clyde Ride has been on the road performing at various venues and accomplishing intricate maneuvers in parades. The team has attended many notable events, including the Tournament of Roses Parade, Calgary Stampede, Pacific National Exhibition, North West Washington Fair, and was awarded "Best Overall Entry" at the Fort Langley May Day Parade in 2006.

In 2004, Wendee Lynn was awarded Langley Chamber of Commerce New Entrepreneur of the Year, a milestone for her personally as Founder and Team Marshall. A year later, she was nominated for Ernst and Young's New Entrepreneur of the Year and honoured with the President's Award from the Horse Council of British Columbia.

Trent Dyrsmid

From training as a military pilot to race car driving, from photocopier sales representative to stockbroker, Trent Dyrsmid knows all about focus, determination and hard work.

While getting his Diploma in Applied Information Technology, he founded his first start-up. A year into the venture, he determined the business wasn't going to succeed, so he shut it down and returned the investor's money and promptly set out to look for another, more viable venture. In July, 2001, Trent founded Dyrand Systems with his life-savings and a business partner. After overcoming financial difficulties with the help of the same angel investor, profits were soon realized. Today, Dyrand provides IT services to customers as far south as California and as far east as Montreal, and has been ranked on *PROFIT* magazine's Hot 50 list for two consecutive years.

Patti Fasan

Patti Fasan is a Certified Ceramic Tile Consultant from the Ceramic Tile Institute of America and has lectured in Europe, the United States, and Canada. Her consulting firm, Professional Attention to Tile Installations (PATTI), focuses on technical expertise, while her stage presence and vibrant personality inspire audiences to maximize their creative potential.

Patti has written articles for dozens of magazines related to her niche market, and presented two papers at the World Congress of Ceramic Tile Quality. Being one of the few women to do this, and working in an almost exclusively male industry, Patti actively supports women in their quest for success in male-dominated industries.

Maureen Fitzgerald

Maureen Fitzgerald, PhD, is a lawyer, mediator and conflict expert. An international speaker, she is the author of six books including *Corporate Circles, One Circle* and *Hiring, Managing and Keeping the Best*. Her company, CenterPoint Conflict & Collaboration Inc., is dedicated to resolving conflict and building trusting teams through facilitation, mediation, training and presentations.

Ken Funk

Ken Funk is the former president and CEO of Golden Valley Foods Ltd., a food manufacturing, wholesale/distribution company employing 160 people. The company was founded in 1950 by Ken's father, and with Ken's leadership, went on to produce sales in excess of one hundred million prior to its sale in 2006.

Ken has earned many accolades for the exponential growth of the company, including Canadian Entrepreneur of the Year award for Agriculture and Food. He has also volunteered as a business consultant for Junior Achievement programs, Big Sisters' "In School Mentoring Program", and was a city councilor in Abbotsford, British Columbia, for three years. He has two children and six grandchildren.

Wally and Dawn Garrick

Owners and operators of the Reel-Inn fishing resort near the shores of Lesser Slave Lake in Faust, Alberta, Wally and Dawn

Garrick live their passion for the outdoors and fishing. They are also the co-founders and former owners of All Weather Shelters, a leading manufacturer and distributor of outdoor mobile shelters.

Eric Huang

Eric Huang, president of J. Easton Capital and Management Consulting Ltd., and owner of China King restaurant, received his MBA in International Finance from Texas A&M International University in Texas. He has been a manager, executive, and entrepreneur in companies and government in China, the United States and Canada. His experience in these roles is diverse, ranging from manufacturing, international trade, retail, restaurant ownership, news publication, IT and corporate finance. He taught business courses at Simon Fraser University and Surrey College, British Columbia. Eric is active in communities, business associations, public speaking, and bridging opportunities between China, Canada, and the United States. He is married to Jessica Zhao and has two kids, Nissen Huang and Lisha Huang.

Azim Jamal

Azim Jamal is a leading inspirational speaker and an international best-selling author. Educated in Kenya, the U.K. and Canada, he made his life-changing career switch from "accounting for business" to "accounting for life" during a soul-stirring experience while volunteering in the developing world. Overcome by the plight of homeless refugees in war-torn areas of the world, he vowed to make a difference in people's lives.

Since then, Azim has been spreading his unique, thought-provoking message on becoming a "Corporate Sufi"—one who can achieve material abundance through spiritual abundance. Over one million people worldwide have heard Azim's inspiring words and his work has received accolades from leading thinkers, including: Dr. Deepak Chopra, Dr. Wayne Dyer, Jack Canfield, Brian Tracy, Seth Godin, and Dr. Ken Blanchard.

Rick and Jacqueline Jongkind

Former struggling small business owners, Rick and Jacqueline Jongkind have spent the past twelve years with a Direct Marketing company. During this time, they have reached the top one percent of income earners in their company and are in the top one percent of income earners in North America. They have earned the prestigious President's Club, have served on the company's field advisory board, and have become some of the most sought after speakers and trainers in the Direct Marketing industry. With no post-secondary education or formal business training, Rick and Jacqueline are an example of what hard work, perseverance, and never giving up on your dreams can provide.

The Jongkind's have been married for 25 years and have five children and six grandchildren. Family, quality of life, great health and contribution have been, and remain, the most important aspects of their lives.

Ozzie Jurock

Ozzie Jurock is president of Jurock Publishing Ltd., and of Jurock International Net Inc., the parent company of FeatureWeb, a Web Development firm and franchise.

Many people, including Peter C. Newman, in his book *Titans*, call Ozzie a "real estate guru". Ozzie is the author of real estate guide, *Forget About Location, Location, Location*, and has published hundreds of real estate articles. He appears every second Wednesday on Global TV News Hour, in Vancouver, BC, to discuss real estate issues. Mark Victor Hansen, co-author of *Chicken Soup for the Soul*, says, "Ozzie is one of the wisest money-men alive," and *Vancouver* magazine called him one of the 45 brightest people in Vancouver.

Peter Legge

Peter Legge lives his dream as an internationally acclaimed speaker, best-selling author, and President and CEO of the largest, independently owned magazine publishing company in Western Canada—Canada Wide Magazines and Communications Ltd. As well as presenting hundreds of keynotes every year, Peter has just published his ninth book, *Make Your Life a Masterpiece*. His keynotes and books have motivated thousands of people towards positive change.

Peter has received countless awards that recognize his business skill, talent and philanthropic endeavours. In 2006, he was awarded the Ambassador of Free Enterprise by Sales and Marketing Executives International in Texas. In 2005, he was presented with the Nido Qubein Philanthropist of the Year Award in Atlanta, Georgia. Toastmasters International voted Peter "Golden Gavel Award Winner" and "Top Speaker in North America", and both the National Speakers Association and the Canadian Association of Professional Speakers have inducted him into the Speakers Hall of Fame.

Ella Little

Ella Little is the owner of Ella's, a British Columbia Lower Mainland boutique renowned for its one-of-a-kind designer clothing and accessories. The first woman to earn Business Person of the Year for the Langley Chamber of Commerce, Ella remains an icon in the business community decades later. In 2006, she celebrated 30 years in business, consistently reaching annual sales of over two million.

Ella's philanthropic endeavours include raising hundreds of thousands of dollars for women's causes and health-related issues. While well known for her community involvement and business acumen, she is most proud of her family: husband, Bob, four children and six grandchildren.

Wendy McClelland

Wendy McClelland is a proud single mom to three young adults and numerous "four-legged friends". She is also a motivational speaker, marketing innovator and Certified Guerilla Marketing Coach who specializes in teaching people to "think without boundaries".

Wendy is a past nominee for Ernst and Young's Canadian Entrepreneur of the Year, and her clients have included software developers, an Olympic athlete and a wide range of business organizations. She has spoken to over ten thousand conference attendees about marketing, Internet business, and motivation.

Darren and Val McDowell

Owners of a start-up in the competitive purified water industry, Darren and Val McDowell have been a thriving presence in Vancouver's Lower Mainland. Just One Drop Water Shops sells bottled spring water and water treatment systems.

In 2003, Darren and Val were recognized by the City of Surrey, British Columbia, with an Entrepreneur of the Year award for their contribution to Surrey's business community. Darren and Val continue to provide personalized service with quality products.

Rob McGregor

Rob McGregor is President of Spirit West Management, Ltd., a management consulting firm based in Vancouver, Canada. He combined his 28 years of expertise in counseling, coaching, and big government change-projects, to co-develop the Smart Team System, a method and tool-set for helping leadership teams master change, conflict, and collaboration.

Rob is a master coach, consultant, chaplain and champion storyteller, holding a B.A. in Psychology, a Master of Divinity, and a Certificate in Conflict Resolution. He works with some of today's most challenging social problems to help leaders understand how to get what they want—stellar business results. He had his paper on the concept of Followership Intelligence (FQ)—the idea that people need to be led in a way they can follow—accepted for the Gallup Institute's 2006 Leadership Summit in Washington, DC.

Harvey McKinnon

Harvey McKinnon started his direct-marketing fundraising company, Harvey McKinnon Associates, in 1989, after working for a decade with Oxfam Canada. Over the years, he has helped raise hundreds of millions of dollars for non-profits across Canada, the US, and overseas.

Author of *Hidden Gold*, the definitive guide to monthly giving, Harvey has a second book entitled *The Tiny Guide To Monthly Giving* (White Lion Press). He produced the acclaimed audio CD, *How Today's Rich Give*, as well as training CD's, videos, and multiple award-winning documentary films that have aired worldwide. Harvey's book, *The Power of Giving*, reached the top five bestseller list on Amazon.com in the US and hit #1 on Amazon.ca. A free downloadable copy is available at www.thepowerofgiving.org . Harvey and his co-author, Azim Jamal, donate all the profits from the sale of this book to non-profit organizations.

Farah Perelmuter

Farah Perelmuter and her husband, Martin, founded Speakers' Spotlight in 1995. Their agency, with offices in Toronto, Calgary and Vancouver, represents and books authors, athletes, politicians, business speakers, comedians, best-selling authors, and other extraordinary personalities, to speak at events world-wide. Their speakers include: the Rt. Honourable Adrienne Clarkson, Justin P.J. Trudeau, Stephen Lewis, the Hon. Preston Manning, Rubin "Hurricane" Carter, Paul Henderson, Michael "Pinball" Clemons, Dr. Roberta Bondar, Cathy Jones, and Ron MacLean.

Farah is listed in Canada's Who's Who, has been featured in numerous national publications, and has twice been nominated as A Woman Who Makes A Difference by *Toronto Life Fashion*. She was also nominated for the Business Development Bank of Canada's Young Entrepreneur Award and the Top Forty Under Forty awards. In 2002, *Chatelaine* nominated Farah for the Rotman Canadian Woman Entrepreneur of the Year Award and she has twice been ranked as one of Top One Hundred Women Business Owners by *PROFIT* magazine.

George Preston

George Preston passed away in January of 2006, a few months after being interviewed for this book. Owner of Preston Chev-

Olds and a business icon and resident in the city of Langley, British Columbia, George employed over 100 people, earning numerous business awards and exceeding sales of 53 million in 2005. Best known for his philanthropic endeavours, George gave tirelessly of his time and money to amateur sport teams, boys' and girls' clubs, music programs and hospital foundations. The Langley Civic Centre was recently re-named the George Preston Civic Centre, in recognition of his giving nature and community commitment.

Laura Prosko

Laura Prosko is the principal founder of Prosko Group Productions Inc., a public relations company specializing in communications and event management for non-profits, political campaigns and the entertainment industry. Her company has raised over $175,000 in three years and garnered media attention, locally, nationally and internationally. Laura has developed her own signature high-profile community events: "Red Ribbon and Rock Gala" AIDS benefit and "Comics for Cancer".

In 2005, Laura was nominated for both *PROFIT* magazine's Top 100 Canadian Women Entrepreneurs and Entrepreneur of the Year at the Inspirational Awards for British Columbia. She is also a professional stand-up comedian and motivational speaker, hosting seminars in Vancouver and Toronto that coach women on entrepreneurship and leadership.

Tami Reilly

As founder and president of GO Get Organized, Tami Reilly has been bringing her unique system of office organization to business owners since 1998. Tami has also developed a do-it-yourself version; The One Day Office Organizer Toolkit brings the power of her system to a fast-growing market segment, the SOHO business owner working from a small office or home office.

Tami was British Columbia's Entrepreneur of the Year, twice, (presented by the prestigious Raymond Aaron Group of Toronto) and is Chair of the Association of Women Business Owners. An experienced and fun presenter with wide media experience, she's been featured on the radio talk show *BizBrainstorm* and played the "Donald Trump" role on *The Job*, an *Apprentice*-type radio show, offering a job at GO Get Organized to the successful contestant.

Susan Rind

Susan Rind, Canadian Designer and owner of Studio Art, specializes in flamework art glass beads. Her work is displayed in art galleries and notable clothing stores across Canada and the U.S. Specific collections have been featured in fashion shows in Vancouver to accent designer clothing such as Escada, Tommy Bahama, and St. John. Susan's art pieces have been showcased in New York City at the Pacific Designer show for two consecutive years, and carried by Coldwater Creek and 60 Nordstrom U.S. stores, including their on-line store. Select groupings of her jewelry are also sold in art galleries in Lahina, Maui, and her work has been published by Sterling Publishing of New York, as part of a coffee table how-to book series sold in Chapters and Michaels.

Mike Robinson

Mike Robinson is co-owner of Ultra Span Structures, creating and selling windbreak and hail protection systems throughout the Americas. As an entrepreneur and Professional Engineer, Mike has lectured and presented proposals in several countries to groups as diverse as farmers, industrial executives, civic building inspectors and engineering associations. He has also fronted two television programs and delivered over 100 talks on the radio. He holds three engineering patents.

Mike is also a certified Communication and Management Skills Coach and District Governor of British Columbia Toastmasters. He has been honoured with a number of awards for speaking and leadership excellence, including Toastmaster of the Year in 2002. He is married and has two children.

Elana Rosenfeld

Elana Rosenfeld is the owner and CEO of Kicking Horse Coffee, Canada's number one Organic and Fair Trade coffee. She and her partner, Leo Johnson, recently celebrated ten years in business and annual sales of eight million. They employ fifteen people in the small Canadian Rocky Mountain town of Invermere, BC.

Kicking Horse Coffee has been featured in many business magazines, including *PROFIT*, and is well known for its branding, creative packaging and ethics.

Brian Scudamore

Brian Scudamore is the Founder and CEO of 1-800-GOT-JUNK? After starting his own junk removal service at the age of eighteen, Brian has gone on to franchise 1-800-GOT-JUNK? in over 250 locations across Canada, the United States and Australia. His leadership is widely recognized by the media and business community.

1-800-GOT-JUNK? is consistently named as one of British Columbia's *Best Companies To Work For* and is ranked as one of America's fastest-growing businesses. Brian has also been featured on *OPRAH*, *FORTUNE* magazine and *CNN*. In his spare time, he contributes a monthly column for *PROFIT* magazine and mentors other young entrepreneurs as a part of Junior Achievement Canada.

Sandra Sereda

Sandra Sereda is co-owner and operator of 34 Little Caesars Pizza outlets in Western Canada. She oversees marketing, promotions, and public relations, and assists in all human resources and operational aspects of the business. She is also the co-owner and operator of Tessa's Pita Chips, a snack food launched in retail stores in Western Canada.

Having a passion for interior design, Sandra is also involved in the purchasing and renovating of high-end homes and the development of a subdivision just outside of Calmar, Alberta, the small Prairie town she grew up in. She is equally passionate about her volunteer work, helping to raise hundreds of thousands of dollars for hospital foundations, "Kids Help Phone", and the Salvation Army.

Alphonse Seward

After helping operate a seventeen-year-old family-owned business that manufactured aluminum windows and installed exterior home improvements, Alphonse Seward made the courageous move to venture into his own business removed from the renovation world. Alphonse Seward, CFP, EPC, has been a practicing Financial Planner with Investors Group since 1996. His success has been largely influenced by dozens of intensive retreats that helped him grow and learn more about different spiritual practices, rituals, psychology, dreams and living-on-purpose.

Alphonse works hard to maintain personal balance in life, engaging in diverse activities like motorcycling, drumming, singing, cooking and traveling. He believes that sharing ordinary time with family and friends gives extraordinary meaning to his life.

Peri Shawn

Peri Shawn teaches and coaches sales VP's and their teams how to take their sales through the roof without taking their sales reps off the job for a single day of training. Peri has taught and coached such diverse executive and sales management teams as Direct Energy, RBC Insurance, Canadian Tire Financial Services and Rogers Wireless.

Known as the Executive Performance Coach, Peri's clients refer to her as the coach's coach. She has been a performance coach for more than ten years. She is the author of sales-coaching articles, coaching books and *The Ultimate Business to Business Sales System*, which includes more than 80 resources for B2B sales managers to increase their sales teams' results.

Terry Smith

Terry Smith established Brewmasters in 1991, a beer and wine brewing company. Six years later, he earned the Langley Chamber of Commerce Business Person of the Year award. Terry also owns several commercial properties in Vancouver's Lower Mainland, improving many of these sites to appeal to the broader community and visitors.

Highly involved in his community since becoming an entrepreneur, Terry was the founding member and chair of the Downtown Merchants Association in Langley, has been elected to city council for seven consecutive years, and has served as the president of the Lower Mainland Municipal Association. He currently chairs the Claims Committee of the Municipal Insurance Association.

John Stanton

Thousands of people have improved their health and fitness levels, lost weight and changed their lives as a result of John Stanton. Founder of the Running Room, John Stanton has grown his company from an 8 x 10 foot store in 1984, to one of North America's largest specialty chains; the Running Room, Coin des Coureurs and Walking Room are located in 87 locations in Canada and the US as of 2006.

John was named to *Maclean's* magazine 2004 Canada Day Honour Roll as one of ten Canadians making a difference in our nation, for his contribution to health through fitness. In 2005, he received the Alberta Centennial Medal in recognition of his service to the people of Alberta. In 2006, he was inducted into the Alberta Business Hall of Fame and received an honorary diploma in Marketing from NAIT, the Northern Alberta Institute of Technology. A best-selling author of three books on running, John is active in community-wide fitness initiatives from Abbotsford, British Columbia, to Moncton, New Brunswick, including the Ambassador for Capital Health.

Brian Takeda

Brian Takeda is the president of INFUZE Holdings Inc., the parent company to the *muzi tea bar* and the *muzi* premium tea line. Brian first developed the socially conscious tea business model as a fourth year graduation thesis at the Queen's School of Business. After graduating in the Spring of 2002, Brian and his business partner, Mars Koo, decided to implement the plan. Within six months, angel investors flocked to the concept and helped the business grow.

In 2005, Brian negotiated a joint venture project with AIYA Corporation, Japan's largest manufacturer of premium Japanese green tea and matcha products, for the exclusive distribution rights for North America. Since then, Brian has been instrumental in the launch of a wide variety of green tea flavored foods and beverages throughout Canada and the United States. As of 2006, over 6000 retailers, cafes, juice bars and restaurants serve matcha.

Sylvia Taylor

Sylvia Taylor is an award-winning freelance writer, editor, instructor, and owner of Taylor-Made Writing Services. Whether supporting others in their self-expression, collaborating in commissioned work or creating insightful commentary and reportage, Sylvia draws on her education, administrative, healthcare, and creative, professional background.

She is editor and chief writer for *The New View*, writes a wide variety of magazine and newspaper articles, business and commissioned works, edits in all genres, and is in her sixth term as Fraser Valley Regional Director for the Federation of British Columbia Writers. She is also an inspiring public speaker and adult educator, teaching creative and non-fiction writing at conferences and writing programs, and judging numerous writing competitions. Her devotion to the arts and women's wellness led to a 2002 nomination for the Women of Excellence awards.

Maureen Wilson

As the owner of the successful Sweat Co. Workout Studios in Vancouver, British Columbia, Maureen is one of Canada's most sought-after and dynamic fitness professionals. She has earned the respect of her peers and gained a dedicated following with her expertise and innovative approach to fitness.

Maureen is an international presenter, ACE-certified personal trainer, instructor and CEC provider, and BCRPA Trainer of Leaders and Spinning instructor. She regularly appears as a fitness expert on television and in print.

Bibliography

(Note: The following resources are also recommended reading.)

Alexander, Graham. 2005. *Tales from the Top: Ten Crucial Questions from the World's #1 Executive Coach*. Nashville: Nelson Business.

Baker, Dan, Greenberg, Cathy, and Collins Hemingway. 2006. *What Happy Companies Know: How the Science of Happiness Can Change Your Company for the Better*. Upper Saddle River: Pearson Education.

Borba, Michele. 1999. *Parents Do Make a Difference: How to Raise Kids With Solid Character, Strong Minds, and Caring Hearts*. San Francisco: Jossey-Bass.

Canfield, Jack with Janet Switzer. 2005. *The Success Principles: How to Get from Where You Are to Where You Want to Be*. New York: HarperCollins.

Chopra, Deepak. 2003. *The Spontaneous Fulfillment of Desire: Harnessing the Infinite Power of Coincidence*. New York: Harmony Books.

Collins, Jim. 2001. *Good to Great: Why Some Companies Make the Leap ... and Others Don't*. New York: Harper Business.

Covey, Stephen. 1989. *The Seven Habits of Highly Effective People: Restoring the Character Ethic*. New York: Simon and Schuster.

Evans, Gail. 2003. *She Wins You Win: The Most Important Strategies for Making Women More Powerful.* New York: Gotham Books.

Fitzgerald, Maureen. 2006. *One Circle: Tapping the Power of Those Who Know You Best.* Vancouver: Quinn Publishing.

Frishman, Rick and Jill Lublin. 2004. *Networking Magic: Find the Best—from Doctors, Lawyers, and Accountants to Homes, Schools, and Jobs.* Avon: Adams Media.

Gerber, Michael. 2001. *The E-Myth Revisited: Why Most Small Businesses Don't Work and What to Do About It.* New York: Harper Business.

Gladwell, Malcolm. 2005. *Blink: The Power of Thinking Without Thinking.* New York: Little, Brown and Company.

Gladwell, Malcolm. 2002. *The Tipping Point: How Little Things Can Make a Big Difference.* New York: Little, Brown and Company.

Helmstetter, Shad. 1982. *What to Say When You Talk to Your Self: Powerful New Techniques to Program Your Potential for Success!* New York: Pocket Books.

Kiyosaki, Robert and Sharon Lechter. 2005. *Rich Dad's Before You Quit Your Job: 10 Real-Life Lessons Every Entrepreneur Should Know About Building a Multimillion-Dollar Business.* New York: Warner Business Books.

Kolbe, Kathy. 2004. *Powered by Instinct: 5 Rules for Trusting Your Guts.* Phoenix: Monumentus Press.

Lowndes, Leil. 2003. *How to Talk to Anyone: 92 Little Tricks for Big Success in Relationships.* New York: Contemporary Books.

Mandino, Og. 1996. *The Greatest Miracle in the World.* Hollywood, FL: Lifetime Books.

Maxwell, John C. 2004. *Winning With People: Discover the People Principles that Work for You Every Time.* Nashville: Nelson Books.

Maxwell, John C. 1993. *Developing the Leader Within You.* Nashville: Thomas Nelson Publishers.

Rath, Tom and Donald O. Clifton. 2004. *How Full is Your Bucket? Positive Strategies for Work and Life.* New York: Gallup Press.

Ruiz, Don Miguel. 1997. *The Four Agreements: A Toltec Wisdom Book*. San Rafael: Amber-Allen Publishing.

Shafir, Rebecca Z. 2000. *The Zen of Listening: Mindful Communication in the Age of Distraction*. Wheaton: Quest Books.

Wiseman, Richard. 2003. *The Luck Factor: Changing Your Luck, Changing Your Life: The Four Essential Principles*. New York: Miramax Books.

About the Author

Karen McGregor, M.Ed., is a professional speaker, author, and communications specialist. An award-winning writer, her work has appeared in national magazines and periodicals, celebrating the practical wisdom of successful entrepreneurs. Holding seminars and keynotes across Canada, Karen helps entrepreneurs communicate effectively, strengthen relationships, and reach clarity about *what matters* in their business and life.

Karen is an authentic speaker with practical, start-today information and inspiring stories.

Her passion for communication and her award-winning performance in management and teaching make her a popular speaker at seminars, retreats, conferences and networking events.

Karen resides in the Lower Mainland of Vancouver, British Columbia, with her husband and two young sons.

To order copies of this book or to receive more information on Karen McGregor's products and services, please visit www.sculptingthebusinessbody.com or call 1-604-533-8395.

About Karen's Keynotes and Seminars

Karen McGregor's Keynotes and Seminars are individualized to meet the needs of your company's conferences, retreats and staff meetings. She specializes in helping groups and individuals build exceptional communication skills and strong relationships. She also works with people seeking clarity and renewed commitment to what matters most in their lives.

What People Are Saying About Karen and her Work

"I would recommend Karen to any organization looking for a knowledgeable and genuine speaker who can impart sound business advice."

Tracie Moser, Founder, www.workshopsforwomen.ca

"I have attended many different seminars and was happy to see that this was FRESH information! It made me stop and think!"

Lori Nordquist, Discovery Toys Manager

"If you want to make your goals a reality, let Karen assist you. She will show you that your goals are not illusive. Through her processes, you will gain a much deeper understanding of what you want to achieve."

Jim Albertson, Chief Officer, BC Ferries Corporation

"Karen handles sensitive topics with respect and with humour. She created an environment that made me feel safe to share my personal stories."

Deanna McIntyre, Creative Memories Consultant

"This seminar 'practiced what it preached'. It was easy to follow, enjoyable and allowed others to take action."

Angela Petersen, West Edmonton Mall
Marine Animal Trainer

To have Karen speak at your next function or to order more copies of this book, please visit her website:

www.sculptingthebusinessbody.com